The Gospel Truth:

"Once Saved, Always Saved" or "Salvation Can Be Lost"

C. A. SHORT

Printed in the United States of America

ROCK SOLID
C. Short Publications
Brentwood, CA
cshortpub@rocksolidbeliever.com

===================================

Summary: An in-depth biblical study on the security of the believer that
includes a thorough study of seldom considered verses,
bringing God's precious truth to light.

ISBN: 978-0989206105

===================================

First Printing, 2014

This book is dedicated to the Lord Jesus Christ who came, died and resurrected that we may know and live in the truth of His Gospel.

1 Cor. 15:1-2
1 Now, brothers, I want to remind you of the gospel I preached to you, which you received and on which you have taken your stand.
2 By this gospel you are saved, if you hold firmly to the word I preached to you. Otherwise, you have believed in vain.

ACKNOWLEDGEMENTS

First of all, I want to give all glory and honor to our Lord Jesus Christ for His unfailing love and unalterable sacrifice. Without His sacrifice, we could never have this marvelous hope of eternal life and the wonderful gift of the Holy Spirit. It is only by the influence, guidance and enabling of the Holy Spirit that this book could ever have been written.

I also thank my wife, Gloria, for her patience and support and my daughters, Kristy and Kelly, for their many hours of proofreading and constructive input. And I want to thank those who read and provided input on "beta" versions of this book as it progressed and all who prayed faithfully that the Holy Spirit would have full control in the writing and production of this book.

With deepest appreciation,

Claude A. Short

CONTENTS

PART III – "ONCE SAVED, ALWAYS SAVED"

Teaching #1: Once a person has a moment of true faith in Jesus Christ, he will always remain saved and cannot again be lost. Such a person is "eternally secure."

Teaching #2: If a professing Christian permanently turns away from Jesus to live in sin, such a Christian was never really saved in the first place...no matter how strong his or her testimony for Jesus was before falling away.
   "Eternal Security" or "Eternal Insecurity"
   A Greater Problem

Teaching #3: The good or bad a Christian does cannot affect his salvation.
   Questions Answered:
   Can a Christian Who Continues to Do Wrong End Up Being a Child of the Devil?
   Is Jesus the Source of Eternal Salvation to Those Who Disobey Him?
   Can a Christian Live by Faith and in Disobedience at the Same Time?
   Do Those Who Willfully Disobey Jesus Love Jesus?

INTRODUCTION

The first 29 years of my life were guided by error-filled doctrine. I was born and raised in a biblically weak denomination that left me empty and searching for answers about life. While in my mid-twenties, I could find no reason for living in this "stupid and painful world" and I needed to talk to God quick. So the search began.

I began my search for a way to talk to God in all the wrong "spiritual" places. Finally, after several years of disappointment in the dangerous world of parapsychology, God, in His infinite love, grace and compassion, led me to His Glorious Son and His wonderful Word.

I finally found the source of all truth...the source that would answer all my questions about life. And having found the truth, I was greatly disturbed that it had been hidden from me for so many years. I have since come to the conclusion that carelessness in teaching God's Word is not only an affront to our Holy God, but is disastrous for believers and nonbelievers alike.

As I grew in the knowledge of God's Word, I discovered that I had been taught a different gospel than the one that was clearly expressed in my already well-used Bible. Now that I had God's Word, I was determined that I would never again allow myself to be duped by any person or false teaching. I also wanted to share what I had discovered with my many friends in the denomination I was raised in.

After two years of trying to reach out with what I had learned in the Bible, my wife and I made a decision to leave our denomination. I was happy that we would finally be going to a Bible-believing church that would be united in God's truth...so I thought.

It wasn't long before I started hearing strange, conflicting ideas about what the Bible says. The most obvious was between those who believed "once saved, always saved" (also known as Unconditional Security) and those who believed that a Christian can forfeit his or her salvation by turning from Jesus to a life of sin (known as Conditional Security). I had heard what men had to say, but I wanted to know the unadulterated truth about salvation and I wanted to see it in the Bible.

It was around 38 years ago that I made my first commitment to go completely through the New Testament just to find out what God really says about these two diametrically opposed doctrines. I have since repeated this process many times, using Greek study helps in order to reach the most accurate biblical conclusion possible. And, as a pastor/teacher, I wanted to be sure I was believing and teaching what God's Word really says. The results of these studies are the substance of this book.

I want to assure you that this book was never intended to be divisive, but to be an exposition of God's truth. It is important that love and unity be maintained among those who truly love Jesus, yet disagree concerning these two doctrines. However, the truth should never be overlooked for the sake of unity. God's will is that we speak the truth in love (Eph. 4:15).

I know and love many wonderful Christians who do not believe as I do. These believers truly love Jesus and hate sin. I continue to enjoy fellowship with them as I look for Spirit-led opportunities to share what I have found in God's Word in a loving and respectful manner. I encourage you to do the same.

Sharing God's pure, unadulterated Word is of eternal importance. I sincerely pray that God will use this book to break down all preconceived, destructive and inaccurate ideas concerning the topics covered in this book, and that He will reveal His truth to all who seek it.

May the Lord Jesus Christ and His Holy Word be glorified!

PART I

LAYING THE FOUNDATION

CHAPTER 1

The Two "Gospels"

I have participated in several denominations and one nondenominational church in my lifetime. Attending these different churches has been quite educational. I have observed that each has beliefs that contradict the others. And, sadly, I have often seen God's Word distorted in an effort to make it fit certain distinctive beliefs.

One of the reasons for many of these contradictions is that there are two different gospel-related doctrines currently being preached in our churches. One is in sync with the gospel that Paul and the Apostles preached and the other is a different "gospel," a misrepresentation of the true gospel that was instituted by God through the blood of Jesus Christ. This is a serious issue that should not be ignored.

Jesus warned His disciples to beware of the yeast of the Pharisees, meaning their false teaching. The problem with yeast is that it works its way completely through the dough, affecting the whole batch. The different "gospel" that is being preached today, like yeast, continues to spread and grow, having a negative and destructive effect on the church as a whole.

Being that the true gospel is the result of the cross of our Lord Jesus Christ, personally searching God's Word to find out which "gospel" is true is every Christian's responsibility. Paul reveals the seriousness of perverting the true gospel by what he said to the Galatian Christians who were embracing a gospel of salvation by legalistic works:

> Gal. 1:6-9
> 6 I am astonished that **you are so quickly deserting the one who called you** by the grace of Christ and **are turning to a different gospel—**
> 7 which is really no gospel at all. Evidently some people are throwing you into confusion and are trying to **pervert the gospel of Christ.**
> **8 But even if we or an angel from heaven should preach a gospel other than the one we preached to you, let him be eternally condemned!**
> 9 As we have already said, so now **I say again**: If anybody is preaching to you a gospel other than what you accepted, **let him be eternally condemned!**

Please do not get me wrong. By including the above passage of scripture, I am not saying that everyone who inadvertently misrepresents the gospel in some points will be eternally condemned. I included the above passage to demonstrate the seriousness of accepting or purposely teaching a distorted gospel. I address the consequences of inadvertently preaching an inaccurate gospel in another chapter.

Galatians 1:6-9 does tell us how deeply Paul felt about any teaching that strays from the pure gospel. And, being that "all Scripture is inspired by God," we also learn how God feels about any perversion of the divine Word given to the Apostles by Jesus Himself. And as Bible-believing, Jesus-loving Christians, we definitely must not tolerate a "different gospel."

Therefore, it is a dangerous practice to accept every doctrine that comes our way without examining each in the light of God's Word. Those who do this are like baby birds waiting to be fed worms by their mother…and sometimes that's what they get…worms! Solely listening to your favorite teacher or denomination does not guarantee that you are getting the pure, unadulterated Word of God. If we want to know the truth, we must study God's Word for ourselves…we must be Bereans (Acts 17:11).

Having two central doctrines that are diametrically opposed has divided the church. God did not give His Word to divide the church, but that we would be of one mind (2 Cor. 13:11), contending for the faith that was once for all entrusted to us (Jude 3).

Therefore, let's do with these two diametrically opposed doctrines what we should do with every teaching we hear. Let's compare each part of them with what God's Holy Word really says.

The Doctrine of Unconditional Security (Once Saved, Always Saved)

The doctrine of Unconditional Security is also known as the Once saved, Always Saved doctrine. It states that once a person truly believes in and receives Jesus as Lord and Savior, he will end up in heaven no matter what he does or how he lives afterward. He is unconditionally secure and cannot be cut off from Jesus nor can he forfeit his salvation.

Proponents of this doctrine also maintain that those who have truly received Jesus, but then turn from Him, are still saved and will eventually come back to Him. If such a person does not return to Jesus, they conclude that he or she was never really saved in the first place.

According to this teaching, once a person believes in and receives Jesus, there is no further condition they must fulfill in order to be welcomed into heaven. This is the gospel without an "if" in it.

The Doctrine of Conditional Security (Salvation Can Be Lost)

The doctrine of Conditional Security states that those who believe in and receive Jesus as their Lord and Savior are eternally secure as long as they abide (remain) in Jesus. The believer must continue in the faith to receive a rich welcome into heaven. Being that Jesus is our Salvation and the only Eternal Life, we must remain in Him to have eternal life.

This doctrine also teaches that it is possible for a believer to fall from grace and to turn from the faith. Those who abandon the faith to live in sin are in danger of being "cut off [from Jesus], thrown into the fire and burned" (John 15:5-6)…that is, unless they repent and return to Jesus before it is too late.

Those who believe in Conditional Security believe that Christians are eternally secure only "if" they remain in Jesus and continue in the faith. Therefore, the condition to Conditional Security is that one must remain in Him to remain in a state of salvation. This is the gospel with an "if" in it.

"If" - The Little Big Word

I am often astonished by how blind I can be while looking in the refrigerator. "Honey, where's the butter?" and the answer comes, "It's right there in front of you," and then my response, "Duuuh…I don't know why I didn't see it." But that's okay, as long as I confine my hurried glances to the refrigerator and don't let this habit carry over to God's Word.

It amazes me how blind we can be to important words in the Bible that are right under our noses. Perhaps it's the result of being too hurried, or perhaps it's from being too presumptuous, assuming that we already understand the text. Whatever the problem is, we often miss the clear meaning of the text because we pass over words as though they are not there…words like "if."

"If" is a little word with a huge meaning. So before we look at the Scriptures to see whether the Apostles taught a Conditional or Unconditional gospel, let's look at the meaning of this incredibly important little word:

Dictionary Definition of "IF": <u>*On the condition that.*</u> *"She will clean the windows only <u>if</u> she is paid."*

GREEK
<u>NT:1487</u> ei) ei (i); *a primary particle of conditionality; if, whether, that, etc.* (Strong's Greek/Hebrew).

When my three daughters were still living at home, if I said, "Hey girls, I'll take you out for pizza tonight 'if' you finish your homework," they had no trouble figuring out that there was a condition to getting that pizza. They knew they would only get the pizza on the condition that they finished their homework.

The purpose of this story is to point out that in our world we readily understand that "if" is a word that puts a condition to what we are being told. However, when reading the Bible, many people overlook this word as though it was not important or like it wasn't even there. This often leads to a misinterpretation of what God is saying.

The Bottom Line

To get to the point, the Unconditional Security gospel is the gospel with no **"if"** in it, and the Conditional Security gospel is the gospel with an **"if"** in it. So the question must be, "Did the Apostles teach the gospel with an **'if'** in it (conditional), or did they teach the gospel with no **'if'** in it (unconditional)?"

The answer to that question will tell us which gospel Paul and the Apostles proclaimed and which they did not.

CHAPTER 2

The Gospel Paul Preached

The pure, unadulterated gospel…the gospel Paul preached…that's what we're after. Changing God's Word, even in the slightest, is like changing the course on your compass by just one little degree. By the end of your voyage you will find yourself way off course and most likely in the wrong country.

This same principle applies to God's Word. Being off in the slightest, especially in the teaching of salvation and eternal security, can throw the whole direction of a Christian's life way off course.

So we must ask, "Did the gospel the Apostles proclaimed teach that salvation can be had for all who truly receive Jesus on the condition that they do not abandon Him? Or did the Apostles proclaim a gospel with no condition at all…one that taught that once you are truly saved what you do or how you live afterward makes no difference to your eternal destination, because once you are saved, you are always saved?"

In other words: Did the gospel that the Apostles proclaimed have an **"if"** in it or not? Let's find out.

The True Gospel

Below is a declaration by the Apostle Paul concerning the gospel that he and the other Apostles proclaimed. In view of the definition of the word **"if,"** I have placed "on the condition that" next to the word **"if"** below for an even clearer understanding of what Paul was saying:

The Gospel Truth

Col. 1:21-23

21 Once you were alienated from God and were enemies in your minds because of your evil behavior.
22 But now **he has reconciled you by Christ's physical body** through death **to present you holy in his sight**, without blemish and free from accusation—
23 **if** [on the condition that] **you continue in your faith**, established and firm, not moved from the hope held out in the gospel. **This is the gospel that you heard and that has been proclaimed** to every creature under heaven, **and of which I, Paul, have become a servant.**

Wow! Look at verse 23. The words **"if you continue in your faith"** are inescapable. In other words, Paul told these "reconciled" believers that God would present them holy in His sight, **"if"** (on the condition that) they continued in their faith.

Some will say, "But the Bible only indicates that the gospel is conditional once, and that's not enough for me." Actually, God only has to say something once for it to be true. However, God tells us that the gospel is conditional many times throughout the Bible. But for now, let's consider the above verses along with the following:

1 Cor. 15:1-2

1 Now, brothers, I want to remind you of **the gospel I preached to you**, which you received and **on which you have taken your stand.**
2 **By this gospel you are saved, if** [on the condition that] **you hold firmly to the word I preached to you. Otherwise, you** have believed in vain.

There it is again. Paul is talking about the gospel he preached and on which the Corinthians had taken their stand. And then, in verse two, he makes it clear that their salvation was conditional by saying, **"By this gospel you are saved, if you**

hold firmly to the word I preached to you. Otherwise, you have believed in vain."

What of those who did not "hold firmly to the word" Paul preached? In verse two, Paul makes it clear that such Christians have "believed in vain." In other words, their faith would become useless, and useless faith, like a useless life preserver, saves no one. So Paul again makes it clear that salvation is conditional on continuing in the faith.

This is the true gospel the Apostles proclaimed...the gospel God has given us the responsibility to uphold:

> Jude 3
> Dear friends, although I was very eager to write to you **about the salvation we share**, I felt I had to write and urge you to **contend for the faith that was once for all entrusted to the saints**.

The Bible makes it clear that every true Christian is considered a saint (one who is set apart to serve Jesus). Therefore, we all have the responsibility of making sure that the gospel Paul and the Apostles preached remains pure by confronting any error brought into it. And, to do this properly, it is important that we pay close attention to the word tenses found in salvation verses of the Bible. Understanding the Greek tenses used in salvation verses will really "turn the lights on" concerning the eternal security issue!

CHAPTER 3

Word Tenses - They Are Very Revealing

At a very young age I learned that word tenses are very revealing. After all, they tell you when something has happened, is happening or will happen. And so we have the past, present and future tenses, which are the basic tenses I remember from school. However, there is a very important fourth tense used in the English language. This tense most closely describes the original Greek in many places, but is vastly ignored by most Bible translations. Understanding this fourth tense and where it should be used in Scripture will open your eyes to some surprising truths about eternal security.

Before we talk about this fourth tense, let's look at some examples of the three most common tenses, using the word "believe." I hope this doesn't seem too much like a simple grammar lesson...it's really important for getting to the truth about the security of the believer.

"He believed." This is the **past tense** use of the word "believe" and it tells us that there was a time when someone once believed. This small sentence does not tell us whether the person is still believing or not, but it does make it clear that this person did believe at some time in the past.

"He believes." This is the **present tense** of the word "believe" and it tells us that someone presently believes. However, it does not tell us whether or not the person will still believe in the future.

"He will believe." This is the **future tense** use of the word "believe" and it tells us that someone is going to believe at some time in the future.

I know this is basic, but because of the way we speak and think, we often miss important biblical truths that the original Greek clearly reveals by using more precise word tenses. Therefore, in order to get the most accurate translation of these tenses, we will be using Young's Literal Translation of the Bible. Stick in there now…Young's Literal Translation will most likely open your eyes to biblical truth you have never seen before.

Young's Literal Translation (YLT Version) - Where the Truth Comes Out

This wonderful translation was originally created in 1862 by Robert Young, a Hebrew and Greek scholar, who also compiled Young's Analytical Concordance. This is an extremely literal translation that preserves the true tenses and accurate word usage found in the original Greek and Hebrew writings.

Robert Young created the "Literal Translation" because of inaccuracies produced in modern versions while translating the Bible into English. These inaccuracies largely occur in the use of word tenses, certain verbs and nouns, and sentence structures. Robert Young felt that the clear inspiration of the original text was being overlooked because of these inaccuracies, voiding much of the Word of God "by the traditions of men."

Being that Young's Literal Translation seeks to preserve the original sentence flow of the Greek, it can be difficult to read. However, it is an important study tool for those who seek the pure truth of God's Word. Using this translation, you can more clearly see what God said and how He said it in the original tenses.

Hang on to your hat…this is very revealing.

What the Bible Really Says About Believing and Salvation

Now let's get to the meat of this chapter and examine a few popular passages in light of their original Greek tenses. Our goal is to answer the following questions:

- How can a person possess salvation and eternal life?
- Does the person who has once truly believed, but has since abandoned the faith still possess eternal life?
- Is it only the person who presently and continually believes and follows Jesus that possesses eternal life?

We will start off with one of the most well-known verses in the Bible taken from the New International Version and then look at the same verse using Young's Literal Translation:

John 3:16
"For God so loved the world that he gave his one and only Son, that whoever **believes** in him shall not perish but have eternal life." NIV

Let's take a good look at this verse while paying close attention to the tenses. In John 3:16 we have the phrase "For God so loved the world," which is past tense. So we know that this verse is talking about God's love as expressed when He gave His Son to die for our sins (Rom. 5:8). And then we have the phrase, "that whoever believes," which is in the present tense, and the phrase "shall not perish," which speaks of the future.

Although this verse uses three tenses, many people only see two. This is because they read "that whoever believes" as though it reads "that whoever has once believed," placing an inaccurate emphasis on a past moment of faith. However, God's Word places the emphasis on present faith, not on a past moment of faith. This verse clearly tells us that it is whoever "believes" right now that has eternal life and shall not perish. And this is important.

If I told you, "My wife keeps a neat house," and you told her I said, "My wife once kept a neat house," that little change in the tense could cause some mighty big problems for me. Not getting the tenses clear always causes problems, and this is especially true when it comes to the Bible.

Now, for even more word-tense accuracy, let's take a look at John 3:16 in the Young's Literal Translation:

> John 3:16
> for God did so love the world, that His Son — the only begotten — He gave, that every one who **is believing** in him may not perish, but may have life age-during. YLT

I am not a Greek scholar, but Robert Young surely was. Young's literal translation gives us the most accurate understanding of this verse by using the words, "is believing" instead of the word "believes," which offers less clarity.

"Is believing" is the fourth English tense I previously referred to (the present continuous tense) and is more in sync with the Greek than "believes." "Is believing" indicates present and continuous action. The point is that the Greek verb in John 3:16 emphasizes that the person who has "life age-enduring" (eternal life) must be presently and continuously believing.

To interpret this verse as though it read, "whoever once believed shall not perish, but has eternal life" is not at all true to the Greek and is a terrible distortion of God's Word. God clearly tells us that whoever is presently and continuously believing has eternal life, which would exclude those who once believed and have since abandoned the faith:

Word Tenses – They Are Very Revealing

1 Tim. 4:1
The Spirit clearly says that in later times **some will abandon the faith** and follow deceiving spirits and things taught by demons.

One of the reasons for the popularity of the once saved, always saved doctrine is that John 3:16 is being taught as though it says, "For God so loved the world that he gave his one and only Son, that whoever **has once believed** in him shall not perish but have eternal life…no matter what they do in the future."

However, when we properly translate the tense in this verse, we find that it does not say that at all. As a matter of fact:

*****

There is absolutely no place in the Bible that indicates that a past moment of faith secures a person's salvation forever, no matter how he or she lives thereafter. Salvation is always indicated, in the original Greek, as being assured only to those who are presently believing in and following Jesus!

*****

No one except God knows the final outcome of each wayward Christian. However, I can say that all who are not presently following Jesus are walking on dangerous ground.

Additional "Present-Continuous-Tense" Salvation Verses

Below, I have included more salvation verses, using the Young's Literal Translation. This is not an exhaustive list, but it should give you a good understanding of what God really says.

I would advise you to acquire your own Young's Literal Translation for further study. This translation can presently be found on the Internet free of charge.

John 3:18
he who is believing in him **is not judged**, but he **who is not believing hath been judged** already, because he hath not believed in the name of the only begotten Son of God. YLT

John 3:36
he who **is believing** in the Son, **hath life age-during**; and **he who is not believing** the Son, **shall not see life**, but the wrath of God doth remain upon him. YLT

John 6:40
and this is the will of Him who sent me, that every one who **is beholding the Son**, and **is believing** in him, **may have life age-during**, and I will raise him up in the last day. YLT

Acts 10:43
to this one do all the prophets testify, that through his name every one that **is believing** in him **doth receive remission of sins**. YLT

Rom. 1:16
for I am not ashamed of the good news of the Christ, for it is the power of God to **salvation to every one who is believing**, both to Jew first, and to Greek. YLT

1 John 5:11-13
11 and this is the testimony, that life age-during did God give to us, and this — the life — is in His Son;
12 he who is having the Son, hath the life; he who is not having the Son of God — the life he hath not.
13 These things I did write to you who **are believing** in the name of the Son of God, that ye may know that life ye have age-during, and that ye may believe in the name of the Son of God. YLT

Word Tenses – They Are Very Revealing

So there you have it...an objective and honest study of salvation verses in their proper tenses. This study should make it clear that truly believing at some time in the past does not guarantee salvation for the person who has since "abandoned the faith" to "follow deceiving spirits and things taught by demons" (1 Tim. 4:1). Once having saving faith does not assure that a person still has saving faith, no more than once having hair guarantees that a person still has hair. Either can be lost.

This may be hard for those who have always believed once saved, always saved to accept. Perhaps one of the reasons for this difficulty is having an inaccurate understanding of what eternal life really is. And who is more qualified to tell us than Jesus Himself?

CHAPTER 4

Eternal Life: What God Says About It

When I was a kid, on a clear summer night, I would lie on the lawn and gaze up at the stars in wonderment. That's when the trouble would begin. I would start thinking, "I wonder where space ends." Then I would try to picture the end of space in my mind's eye, and that would always throw me into mental overload.

Well, I just couldn't get it, and I don't think anyone can. The idea of never-ending or eternal space is just too much for the finite mind to grasp, but we must acknowledge that it exists. However, I have no problem accepting the idea of never-ending life. Perhaps that's because Jesus tells us exactly what it is…and that's all that counts…what Jesus says about eternal life.

Jesus' Definition of Eternal Life

Most Christians think eternal life is just living for an infinite measure of time in heaven. After all, eternity is forever. Right? That is true, however, that is not how Jesus defines eternal life. His definition is not expressed in terms of a measurement of time, but in terms of a relationship with Him.

Jesus said:

John 17:3
"Now **this is eternal life**: that they may know you, **the only true God, and Jesus Christ**, whom you have sent."

So Jesus' definition of eternal life is knowing Him.

A Biblical Definition of Eternal Life: To know Jesus. To have an ongoing, personal and meaningful relationship with Jesus Christ as your Lord and Savior, with you as His servant/follower.

Living forever is the result of this personal relationship.

Eternity is a very long time. Everyone will exist eternally somewhere. Yes, there is eternal life in Jesus, but there is also such a thing as eternal death. Eternal death is existing forever outside of Jesus in a place of eternal suffering (Mark 9:47-48).

Before I came to Jesus, I was terrified at the thought of death. I had heard of heaven and hell, but I was not positive that either existed. And if there was a heaven and hell, I was pretty sure I would end up in the latter. If not, I figured I would die, worms would eat my body and that would be the end of me. None of these options were pleasant to think about and millions of people today face this same dilemma.

Therefore, life after death is the most serious issue we can face. What we believe and teach about eternal life can have a huge impact on where we, and those we share with, end up for eternity. So, let's dig a little deeper into God's Word to see what else God says about eternal life.

Where Eternal Life Is Not Found

The other day one of my daughters lost her keys and, after two days of searching, she called and asked if I would pray with her to find them.

The Lord is so incredible. I kid you not, in less than two minutes after hanging up she called back to say, "Daddy, I found them!" Well, after our little prayer, the Lord led her to look in the right place, and, what do ya know, there were her keys, hanging in the keyhole in the tailgate of her car. Looking in the wrong places got her nowhere.

Likewise, looking in the wrong places for eternal life will get you nowhere and can lead to eternal disaster. Therefore, I want to assure you that you will not find eternal life in a church, denomination, doctrine, human leader, systems of good works, or any other such things. These are all the wrong places. Eternal life can be found in only one place:

> 1 John 5:11-12
> 11 And this is the testimony: God has given us **eternal life**, and **this life is in his Son**.
> **12 He who has [Greek: "is having"] the Son has life; he who does not have the Son of God does not have life.**

> Rom. 6:23
> For the wages of sin is death, but the gift of God is **eternal life in Christ Jesus our Lord**.

The above verses reveal two important truths. They tell us who has eternal life (1 John 5:12) and they tell us the only place where eternal life can be found (verse 11 and Romans 6:23). And so, only he who "is having" the Son has eternal life, for this life is found "in the Son" and nowhere else. Therefore:

<u>Eternal Life is a Precious Gift That is Found Only in Jesus</u>

Now, suppose you offered me one of your CDs...the one called "The Jesus CD." And I said, "Thanks! But I really don't want everything that's on that CD. I'll just take this one song and you can keep the CD and the rest of the songs that are on it." I think you would say, "Sorry, buddy...it's all or nothing. If you don't receive the CD, you can't have the song you want, which is embedded in it, either. And if you want that song, you must receive the CD and everything else that's on it. You can't receive just part of the CD." Simple logic.

Well, oddly enough, some people do not apply this simple logic when it comes to Jesus. There are people who want eternal life, but do not want Jesus, the One it is imbedded in. And there are others who want the Savior part of Jesus, but not the Lord part. However, the Bible makes it clear that we must have Jesus, who is both Lord and Savior, to have the life that is in Him. It's all or nothing…you can't receive just part of Jesus.

Jesus is our Source of Eternal Life, our Lord, our Master, our Peace, our Hope and all we need for life and godliness. Only those who receive Him as Lord and Savior have all that is in Him.

Eternal Life Is the Result of Believing in Jesus

Of course, every Christian knows that you must have faith in Jesus to be saved. However, according to James 2:14-26, there are two kinds of faith. There is faith that saves and there is faith that does not save. One is living faith and the other is dead faith. One produces action and the other produces nothing. One is powerful and the other is meaningless.

Being that saving faith produces action and obedience (Rom. 1:5), all who truly have saving faith are also living for Jesus. It is this living faith that God is talking about in the Gospel of John:

> John 3:16
> For God so loved the world that he gave his one and only
> Son, that whoever **believes [Greek: "is believing"]** in
> him shall not perish but have eternal life.

This Greek tense tells us that our believing must be happening presently and continuously to have eternal life. Faith of the past that has not continued into the present is not living faith…it is faith that was alive, but is now dead.

Eternal Life: What God Says About It

There is a lot of difference between having been wet because I once stood in the rain and staying wet because I am presently and continuously standing in the rain. Standing in the rain once upon a time does not make one wet now. Neither does believing once upon a time make one saved now.

Notice that no translations render John 3:16 as "for God so loved the world that he gave his one and only Son, that whoever **"once believed"** in him shall not perish but have eternal life." There are no versions that would dare translate the above verse using the past tense, "believed." That would be a harmful distortion of the true meaning of the Holy Scriptures. And so, eternal life is the result of presently and continually believing in and having a personal relationship with Jesus Christ as your Lord and Savior.

It was very important to Jesus that His disciples had a clear understanding of what eternal life is. But what about the subject of eternal security? Why is there so much division over whether salvation can be forfeited or not? Is it because Jesus was too vague on this most important subject? Absolutely not! As you will see, what Jesus said about the security of the believer couldn't be clearer.

CHAPTER 5

The True Vine – What Jesus Teaches About Eternal Security

I'm not the greatest gardener…especially when it comes to vegetables. I have planted tomatoes, radishes, carrots and a few other things that did okay, but how those "green-thumbers" get the results they get is beyond me.

I may not know the secrets for getting the best results from plants, but there is one gardening tip I am sure of. If a branch is not well connected to the plant, that branch will not produce good fruit, and, in time, will dry up and die. I also know that it is necessary to cut off diseased or fruitless branches before their pathetic condition affects other branches.

In John chapter 15 Jesus uses this same common-sense gardening approach to give us the truth about eternal security. I love how clearly Jesus presents this truth using the vine and its branches as an example.

I believe John 15:1-6 to be one of the most important and powerful passages in the Bible, for it concerns our relationship with Jesus. Jesus spoke these words to His disciples shortly before He was to be crucified, which makes them most serious. They contain a beautiful promise and a stern warning, so let's dig into this rich spiritual soil and reap a harvest of truth.

Out of the Mouth of Jesus - The Truth About Eternal Security

John 15:1-6

1 "I am the true vine, and my Father is the gardener.
2 He cuts off every branch in me that bears no fruit, while every branch that does bear fruit he prunes so that it will be even more fruitful.
3 You are already clean because of the word I have spoken to you.
4 Remain in me, and I will remain in you. No branch can bear fruit by itself; it must remain in the vine. Neither can you bear fruit unless you remain in me.
5 I am the vine; you are the branches. If a man remains in me and I in him, he will bear much fruit; apart from me you can do nothing.
6 If anyone does not remain in me, he is like a branch that is thrown away and withers; such branches are picked up, thrown into the fire and burned."

In order to provide the clearest understanding of Jesus' teaching on the True Vine, let's take one verse at a time:

John 15:1
1 **I am the true vine**, and **my Father is the gardener**.

Jesus begins this teaching by telling us who He is in relationship to His followers. He is the "True Vine" who gives life to His followers, who are later called His "branches." So, whatever a vine is to a branch, Jesus is to those who love and follow Him.

Jesus also refers to His Father as the Gardener. And what does a Gardener do? The Gardener oversees all things concerning the plants and makes sure they stay healthy, clean and productive. Therefore, the Gardener must often prune back healthy branches and cut off nonproductive ones:

The True Vine

2 He [the Father] **cuts off every branch <u>in me</u> that bears no fruit**, while every branch that does bear fruit he prunes so that it will be even more fruitful.

The natural branch's life depends on its connection to the vine. It is through this union that branches receive everything they need to live and to produce good fruit. This is also true of the Christian life. If we are to receive the life-giving sap of the Holy Spirit, we must be tightly bound to Jesus, our True Vine. Apart from Him we can do nothing, just as a natural branch can do nothing apart from being connected to its vine.

Now there is something in verse two that we must not miss. Jesus tells us that there are branches presently <u>in Him</u> that the Father will cut off from Him for failing to bear fruit. These branches must represent Christians, for it is impossible to be "in" Jesus without being a born-again Christian. Those who are in Jesus are saved and those who are not in Jesus are not saved. Those who are cut off from Him were saved, but are no longer.

Despite this fact, there are still those who will say, "These branches cannot be believers, because once a person is saved, he cannot lose his salvation." Sadly, they inadvertently reject what Jesus clearly said in order to cling to what they already believe…and they do so at the expense of God's truth.

Taking this approach is basically saying that Jesus could not possibly mean what He clearly said because it does not match what I already believe. This is an unhealthy approach to God's Holy Word that can produce terrible consequences.

Jesus makes it clear that those who do not maintain an obedient, love-relationship with Him will, in God's time, be cut off from Him for failing to bear the fruit God desires…that is unless they repent of their waywardness. And what of the healthy, productive branches? Verse two tells us that God prunes (works in) these believers so they "will be even more fruitful."

Let's go on:

3 You are already clean because of the word I have spoken to you.

God's Word cleanses and purifies those who come to and follow Jesus.

4 Remain in me, and **I will remain in you.** No branch can bear fruit by itself; it must remain in the vine. **Neither can you bear fruit unless you remain in me.**
5 I am the vine; **you are the branches. If a man remains in me** and I in him, **he will bear much fruit; apart from me you can do nothing.**

Notice that Jesus uses the word "remain" six times in verses 1-6, five of them being in the two above verses, so it must be extremely important. According to the WordWeb dictionary, the word "remain" means: "Be in an unchanged state for a long time." In other words, it means to "stay" where you already are.

We had a dog named Buddy. He was a Bichon Frisé, and he was wired! "Stay" was one of the most difficult commands for him to obey. "Run," "hop," and "bark," he had no problem with. But it was almost impossible for him to sit still unless he was in my lap, where he loved to be.

Sometimes I would tell Buddy to "stay" in my lap, so that he would not leave and jump all over guests who were entering our home. Now wouldn't it be foolish of me to tell Buddy to remain in my lap if he were not already in my lap? He could only remain in a place where he already was.

In the same way, we can be sure that when Jesus tells His "branches" to "remain" in Him, that He is speaking to those who are already in Him and, thus, are born-again Christians. Likewise, it is obvious that Jesus would not tell believers to remain in Him, if it were not possible for them to abandon Him.

Now, suppose I locked my dog Buddy up in the bedroom and then shouted through the door, "Stay there Buddy…don't you leave that bedroom." I think that if my wife caught me doing that, she might call the men in white coats to lock me up! It makes no sense to tell someone to remain in a place that is impossible to get out of. Therefore, Jesus would never tell Christians to remain in Him if it were not possible for them to desert Him.

The "branches" that Jesus commands to "remain" in Him definitely represent believers who have the freedom to leave or abandon Him any time they choose.

In verse five, Jesus also emphasizes that "apart from" Him we "can do nothing." We must remain in Him through a trusting and obedient relationship or…

> 6 **If** anyone does not remain in me, he is like a branch that is thrown away and withers; **such branches are picked up, thrown into the fire and burned**.

Did Jesus really say that? Straight from the mouth of Jesus comes the truth about eternal security. Jesus tells us that those who fail to remain in Him will spiritually wither, be "picked up, thrown into the fire and burned."

Christians who abandon Jesus to pursue the desires of the sinful nature are in grave danger of eternal disaster. Only God knows the "cut off" point for each person, so those who do not maintain a strong relationship with Jesus are like branches dangling in the wind, just holding on by a mere splinter of bark. To tell wayward Christians that they are secure in Jesus because of a past moment of faith is helping them to their eternal demise. They need to grasp onto Jesus by weaving every fiber of their being back into Him before it is too late.

I would advise any Christian who is not where he or she should be with Jesus to return to Him without hesitation. Why sit on the tailgate while riding on a bumpy road when you can snuggle up in the cab where you are safe and secure?

It can be eternally harmful to distort such clear instructions and warnings from the Lord of lords. To tell Christians who are willfully sinning that they cannot be cut off from Jesus and "thrown into the fire and burned" is to give them a false hope that can lead them to hell.

Those who maintain a servant-Lord relationship with Jesus need not fear falling away...the power of the Holy Spirit flows from the True Vine into our lives, helping us to stand strong in Jesus, who is our only source of security. When we do stumble, we can confess our sins, repent and continue walking with Him.

Those who cling to Jesus enjoy His peace as they walk in His power. Aside from Him there is no peace...there is no power... and there is no salvation. But as we remain in Jesus, we have all He has to offer. This is a glorious life! I am eternally secure as I remain in Jesus!

Over the years, I have heard many false ideas about Conditional Security. Because of these misconceptions, many Christians are actually afraid to believe what Jesus clearly says about it. So, in order to clear up these misconceptions, let's take a quick look at what it's really like for a biblically solid Christian to believe that it is possible for wayward Christians to forfeit their salvation. By the way, I have believed this for 41 joy-filled years, and I have never feared for my salvation.

Clearing Up False Ideas About Conditional Security

I have heard more than a few Christians, usually teachers, paint an inaccurate picture of those who believe salvation can be forfeited. They picture those who believe in Conditional Security as walking around biting their fingernails each time they stumble into some sin, constantly wondering if they are still saved. For those who understand God's Word and promises, this could not be farther from the truth.

The Glorious Life a Saved Person Lives

The person who properly understands Conditional Security also understands that not only are we assured of eternal life <u>in</u>

The True Vine

Christ Jesus, but that we also receive all the good God has for us as we remain in Him:

- We are "alive to God in Christ Jesus" (Rom. 6:11)
- We have "eternal life in Christ Jesus" (Rom. 6:23)
- "There is no condemnation for those who are in Christ Jesus" (Rom. 8:1)
- The love of God is found "in Christ Jesus" (Rom. 8:39)
- We are "sanctified in Christ Jesus" (1 Cor. 1:2)
- We receive God's grace "in Christ Jesus" (1 Cor. 1:4)
- We receive wisdom from God, righteousness, holiness and redemption "in Christ Jesus" (1 Cor. 1:30)
- We have freedom from the Law of Moses "in Christ Jesus" (Gal. 2:4)
- We are sons of God through faith "in Christ Jesus" (Gal. 3:26)
- We are seated in the heavenly realms "in Christ Jesus" (Eph. 2:6)
- We receive God's incomparable riches of grace and kindness "in Christ Jesus" (Eph. 2:7)
- "We are God's workmanship, created in Christ Jesus" (Eph. 2:10)
- We are brought near to God "in Christ Jesus" (Eph. 2:13)
- We find God's purpose for our lives fulfilled "in Christ Jesus" (Eph. 3:11)
- We find the peace of God "in Christ Jesus" (Eph. 4:7)
- God meets all our needs "according to His glorious riches in Christ Jesus" (Phil. 4:19)
- We receive abundant grace, faith and love "in Christ Jesus" (1 Tim. 1:14)
- The promise of life is found only "in Christ Jesus" (2 Tim. 1:1)
- Salvation is only "in Christ Jesus" (2 Tim. 2:10)

So we see that our security, and everything else we need, is not in a doctrine, but in the person of Jesus Christ. Instead of worrying about "losing our salvation," we stand firmly secure in Him, knowing that Satan and all his demons cannot tear us away from Him.

Those who "remain" in Jesus are as safe and secure as can be. Those who are foolish enough to abandon Him for any reason can expect nothing but misery and eternal destruction, for outside of Jesus there is no salvation nor eternal life. We understand that to abandon Jesus for a life of willful sin is to invite spiritual and eternal disaster (Rom. 8:12-14), and the Holy Spirit uses this understanding to keep us focused and dependent on Jesus while being careful not to take sin lightly.

Being that Jesus suffered terribly to cleanse us and to destroy the power of sin in our lives, how can we help but seek to avoid and hate even the slightest hint of sin (Eph. 5:3)? The possibility of forfeiting salvation is not an issue with earnest Christians who believe in Conditional Security…that is unless they begin to compromise their faith by willfully embracing sin. In that case, they'd best repent.

I know that I am eternally secure as I remain in Jesus, who is my Salvation, my Life, my Peace, my Joy, my King, my Master, and the Source of all I need. Praise His holy name!

Jesus' teaching on the True Vine is probably the clearest passage on the subject of salvation and eternal security in the Bible. And there are many other passages that coincide with this teaching, including John 10:27-29, where Jesus tells us that no one can snatch those who listen to and follow Him out of His hand.

However, many who embrace the once saved, always saved doctrine, use this passage to support their belief, saying, "Jesus said, 'No one can snatch <u>us</u> out of His hand?'" But did Jesus really say that?

CHAPTER 6

Who Cannot Be "Snatched" Out of Jesus' Hand?

Talking to those who believe once saved, always saved is always interesting, although the conversation usually goes pretty much the same. "So you don't believe a Christian can walk away from Jesus and forfeit his salvation?" and the reply comes, "No, I don't. I'm in Jesus' hand, and He said that no one can snatch us out of His hand. Besides, I'm a child of God. Does your child cease to be your child just because he goes astray?"

By the way, the idea that a Christian cannot cease to be a child of God, no matter what he does or how he lives, comes from making the same mistake Nicodemus made...looking at the spiritual birth as though it were a natural birth (John 3:3-6).

Now, let's look at the question presented in the title of this chapter this way. Jesus used His precious blood to pay for the ticket that got us on His salvation ship...our salvation did not come cheap. We trusted in Him, received His gracious offer and are now safely on board, headed for eternal life "in the age to come" (Mark 10:30). And so, to put our question another way, "Is it possible for a Christian to abandon the ship of eternal life?"

Let's see what the Bible says:

Who Are Safely in God's Hand?

There is no doubt that those who listen to and follow Jesus are safely tucked away in His hand:

John 10:27-29
27 **My sheep listen to my voice**; I know them, and **they follow me.**
28 **I give them eternal life**, and **they shall never perish**; **no one can snatch them out of my hand.**
29 My Father, who has given them to me, is greater than all; **no one can snatch them out of my Father's hand.**

This, indeed, is a wonderful promise. However, does Jesus really say that no one can snatch "us" out of His hand in verse 28? No, He does not. And you say, "Huh?" Well, read it again and you will see that Jesus does not use the all-inclusive word "us," but the selective word "them," referring only to those who are presently listening to His voice and following Him. Therefore, this promise is not for Christians who have abandoned His protective hand to live according to the sinful nature, which always brings spiritual death (Rom. 8:13).

However, while discussing the once saved, always saved doctrine with those who believe it, most insist that "Jesus said no one can snatch <u>us</u> out of His hand." When asked what they mean by "us," it becomes clear that they mean all Christians, including those who are ignoring Jesus' voice and are not presently following Him. It is as though they interpret these verses as though Jesus said:

27 "My sheep are saved whether they are presently listening to my voice or not; I know them, but they don't have to follow me to have eternal life.
28 I give eternal life to my sheep, even if they have turned from me, and they shall never perish because it is impossible for them to choose to walk out of my hand.
29 My Father, who has given them to me, is greater than all; it is impossible for them to walk out of my Father's hand." EMUV (Extremely Messed Up Version)

Who Cannot Be "Snatched" Out of Jesus' Hand?

Of course, that is not what Jesus said. It is true that Jesus gives eternal life to certain people. And it is also true that those who have this life shall never perish. And it is equally true that no one can snatch these same people out of Jesus' hand. So the real questions should be:

"Who does Jesus give eternal life to and who shall never perish?" "Who cannot be snatched out of Jesus' hand?" and "What about those who choose to walk out of Jesus' hand?"

Let's answer these questions one by one:

1. Who does Jesus give eternal life to and who shall never perish?

Jesus answers this question in verses 27-28:

> **27 My sheep listen to my voice**; I know them, and **they follow me.**
> **28 I give** them **eternal life**, and they **shall never perish; no one can snatch** them **out of my hand.**

First of all, Jesus makes it clear who His sheep are. He tells us that His sheep are those who listen to His voice and follow Him (verse 27). Jesus also tells us that it is those who listen to His voice and follow Him that shall never perish (verse 28). That's what Jesus said, and it's always very important to understand exactly what He said.

However, it is equally important to understand what Jesus did not say. Jesus did not say that those who had once received Him, but now ignore His voice and no longer follow Him shall have eternal life and shall never perish. He also did not say that it is impossible for a person to walk out of His hand if he or she so chooses. The great promises in these verses are specifically for those who are listening to and following Jesus.

This is about the time someone will say, "Well, I believe that those who turn from Jesus were never really saved in the first place." I have heard this many times, often from very sincere Christians. However, the problem with that idea is that it is not taught anywhere in the Bible and, therefore, is unbiblical. Personally, I would not want to share anything that is not clearly taught in the Bible, especially when eternity is at stake.

Sheep who have turned away from Jesus had best repent before they stray completely from His hand. Listen to what Jesus said to the wayward Christians in the church of Laodicea:

> Rev. 3:15-20
> 15 I know your deeds, that you are neither cold nor hot. I wish you were either one or the other!
> 16 So, **because you are lukewarm** — neither hot nor cold - **I am about to spit you out of my mouth**.
> 17 You say, 'I am rich; I have acquired wealth and do not need a thing.' But you do not realize that you are wretched, pitiful, poor, blind and naked.
> 18 I counsel you to buy from me gold refined in the fire, so you can become rich; and white clothes to wear, so you can cover your shameful nakedness; and salve to put on your eyes, so you can see.
> 19 Those whom I love I rebuke and discipline. So be earnest, and **repent**.
> 20 **Here I am! I stand at the door and knock. If anyone hears my voice and opens the door, I will come in and eat with him, and he with me**.

Obviously, these lukewarm Christians were not listening to and following Jesus as they should. As a result, Jesus' words to them were very strong: "I am about to spit you out of my mouth." Actually, the Greek word for "spit" here literally means to "vomit" (Strong's Greek/Hebrew). Not a pretty picture.

I find it interesting that, while talking to these Laodiceans, Jesus also said, "Here I am! I stand at the door and knock. If anyone hears my voice and opens the door, I will come in and eat with him, and he with me." The question is: What was Jesus doing on the outside of their hearts, wanting to come in?

These Laodiceans had allowed their worldly desires to push Jesus out of their hearts. Therefore, Jesus beckoned them to "be earnest and repent" of their wayward ways, or they would be "vomited" out of His mouth. Even if we tone down the original meaning of the Greek and use the word "spit," it still means to "eject." And so Jesus is talking about ejecting those who are lukewarm from Himself.

Jesus obviously finds lukewarmness repulsive and wants us to feel the same way about it. The only solution to this church's pathetic condition was to "repent," return to and follow Jesus as they should. Repentance is a decision to make an about-face and go in the opposite spiritual direction. It is impossible to follow after Jesus and the sinful nature at the same time.

My wife and I were once traveling with some other Christians when one of them began to share about a "born-again Christian" who was willfully living in sin. When I asked how that could be, this person responded, "She has received Jesus as her Savior, but she has not yet received Him as her Lord." This concept is very puzzling, especially being that the idea of receiving Jesus as Savior without receiving Him as Lord cannot be found in God's Word.

Jesus is both Lord and Savior. When a person receives Jesus, he or she must receive Him as He is. You cannot split Jesus in half and say, "Oh, I want to go to heaven, so I think I will just receive Jesus as my Savior, and maybe I will get around to receiving the Lord part after I have had my fling in this world." No! All who come to Jesus should understand that they must receive all of Him or they have none of Him. To refuse to follow Jesus as the Lord of your life is to walk out of His protective hand.

Listening to Jesus' voice and following Him does not mean never sinning, but it does mean hating sin and doing your best to avoid it by the power of the Holy Spirit who lives in you. We all "stumble in many ways" (James 3:2), and God has made provision for that.

However, He gives many stern warnings for those who choose to live in sin rather than to follow Jesus.

It is clear in John 10:27-29 that only those who listen to and follow Jesus have eternal life and shall never perish, not those who are ignoring Him and living in willful sin.

Now, let's move on to the second question:

2. Who cannot be snatched out of Jesus' hand?

Let's look at John 10:27-29 again:

> John 10:27-29
> 27 **My sheep listen to my voice**; I know them, and **they follow me**.
> 28 **I give them eternal life**, and **they shall never perish**; **no one can snatch** <u>them</u> **out of my hand**.
> 29 My Father, who has given them to me, is greater than all; **no one can snatch** <u>them</u> **out of my Father's hand**.

Of course, I totally agree with these verses. That's what God's Word says. Satan and all his demons cannot snatch away those who listen to and follow Jesus.

Now, before going on, it is important to remember that false doctrine often comes from lifting verses, or parts of verses, out of biblical context. In this case, the full context of this verse is seldom quoted, and that which is "quoted" is often misquoted.

When people say, "Jesus said that no one can snatch **us** out of His hand," they make it unclear who Jesus is specifically talking about. However, Jesus clearly qualified who cannot be snatched out of His hand, by saying, "...**no one can snatch** <u>**them**</u> **out of my hand**." So we must again ask, "Who is the 'them' He is referring to?"

The "them" Jesus was talking about is clearly those who are listening to His voice and following Him (verse 27), which

Who Cannot Be "Snatched" Out of Jesus' Hand?

excludes those who are not. To say that this promise applies to all Christians, whether they are listening to and following Jesus or not, is to distort God's Holy Word. And it is sad that this distortion is often used to give false comfort and assurance to Christians who have strayed from Jesus' hand to follow after sin, which brings us to the last question:

3. What about those who choose to walk out of Jesus' hand?

I don't know about you, but I am glad that God left my will in tact after I was saved. That means I can love and follow Him of my own free will. It also means that I can walk away from Jesus in pursuit of worldly pleasures any time I desire. Jesus draws people to Himself by His love, but He will never force a person to love and follow Him.

The other day I was talking to someone who I have known for a very long time. This person used to be on fire for the Lord. He had led at least one person that I know to the Lord, and that person is still following Jesus today. However, the one I was talking to has been living in sin for a very long time and even told me that he just didn't want to live the Christian life anymore. I have no doubt that he had truly received Jesus, yet he is no longer listening to Jesus' voice nor is he following Him. As a result, this man is no longer safely in Jesus' hand. No one snatched or forced him out of Jesus' hand, he simply walked away from Jesus and now his eternal future is looking very grim.

Those who once received Jesus, but have since stopped listening to and following Him, have abandoned Him of their own free will, and, as a sad result, they have also abandoned the eternal life that is found only in Him.

That's why God gives Christians so many warnings concerning their walk...warnings such as:

Gal. 5:19-21
19 **The acts of the sinful nature are obvious**: sexual immorality, impurity and debauchery;

51

20 idolatry and witchcraft; hatred, discord, jealousy, fits of rage, selfish ambition, dissensions, factions
21 and envy; drunkenness, orgies, and the like. **I warn you,** as I did before, that **those who live like this will not inherit the kingdom of God.**

Notice that Paul warned these Galatian Christians that, if they were to live according to the sinful nature and willfully practice the sins mentioned in these verses, they would not "inherit the kingdom of God." There are many more warnings like this that are covered in another chapter, but, for now, let's just remember that the acceptance of any sin in our lives is just the first step of walking out of Jesus' hand.

Christians are not perfect, but God's Word instructs them to aim for perfection (2 Cor. 13:11). They sometimes sin, but are not slaves to sin (Rom. 6:6). As born-again believers, we are to be filled with the Holy Spirit who empowers us to live for Jesus, and we are not to live for the sinful nature. When we do sin, we hate it, repent of it, and confess it to receive God's gracious forgiveness. When we fall, we get up, dust ourselves off and keep going for Jesus, who cleanses us from all unrighteousness (1 John 1:9).

Those who truly love Jesus seek to avoid sin and to live in obedience to Him (John 14:21-24)…and they can know they are eternally secure as they remain in Him.

Jesus is our hope! Jesus is our strength! Jesus is our salvation! Jesus is our security! Jesus is our only place of safety! The righteous will run into Him and be safe (secure). Outside of Him there is no security.

Christians who trust in and cling to Jesus do not have to worry about falling away. Jesus will keep them safe. However, those who choose the world and sin over Jesus should worry, for there is no salvation or security apart from Him.

But what about Paul's "Wretched Man" (Rom. 7:9-25)? How does he fit in with God's plan for Christian victory and salvation? Does he really represent the normal Christian, as some claim he does? Or does he represent someone who is living according to the sinful nature or the law, as others claim?

CHAPTER 7

Paul's "Wretched Man"

Before coming to Jesus I was one wretched man! What I mean is that I was empty, depressed and looking for answers concerning this "stupid, meaningless life." I was raised in a church that did not teach the Bible, but I really wanted to please God. However, no matter how hard I tried, I could not live the way I perceived God wanted me to live. I just kept doing the bad I did not want to do and I was unable do the good I wanted to do on anything close to a regular basis. That was before Jesus gave me new life.

While I was still in that miserable, unsaved state, I heard Jesus' call: "Come to me and I will give you rest for your soul and replace your wretchedness with love, peace and joy as you surrender your life to me."

Jesus promised me a blessed life, not a wretched life…and that He would enable me to crucify the sinful nature along with its passions and desires (Gal 5:24). He also told me He would make me into a new creation and that, step-by-step, year-by-year, He would conform me more and more into His likeness.

2 Cor 5:17
Therefore, **if anyone is in Christ, he is a new creation; the old has gone, the new has come!**

Rom 8:29
For **those God foreknew he also predestined to be conformed to the likeness of his Son,** that he might be the firstborn among many brothers.

Now, if the above scriptures are true, and if God's promises are good, how is it that so many Christians believe that Paul's "Wretched Man" could possibly describe the normal Christian life? The description of Paul's "Wretched Man" is found in Romans 7:9-25, and what a wretched man he is. He is powerless to live the life that God has given us the power to live. He is the perfect picture of what I was <u>before</u> I came to Jesus, which is the opposite of what God says His children should be.

Yet many believers use Romans 7:9-25 to comfort Christians who are struggling with sin. They say something like, "You see how Paul could not keep from doing wrong (Rom. 7:18-19). If sin had such control over Paul, sin must be a normal part of the Christian life. So don't let your sin get you down...we are all weak because we are in the flesh." Weak? In the flesh? Slavery to sin a normal part of our lives? Is that what Jesus died for... that we would be just as weak and wretched after coming to Him as before we came to Him?

Although some use Paul's wretched man in this way, there are many Christians, including myself, who reject the idea that Paul was portraying the normal Christian life in the slightest. And we reject this idea for a very good reason.

A careful examination of Romans 7:9-25, in context with its surrounding chapters, will clearly reveal that Paul was using the wretched man to give a picture of what it was like for him to try to please God while he was still living under the law and under the control of the sinful nature. Therefore, Paul's wretched man is simply a picture of anyone who is living outside of God's glorious plan for His children (Rom. 8:3-4). Paul's speaking in the first person and present tense was simply what some call a "literary device" sometimes used by communicators to better relate to the hearers and was not designed to give a picture of what God intends for the Christian life.

<u>Paul's "Wretched Man" Versus the Spiritually Healthy Born-Again Christian - A Comparison</u>

Paul's Wretched Man

As I have already stated, Paul's wretched man is in no way a picture of God's plan for the normal Christian life. So, in order to clearly demonstrate this truth, let's spend some time comparing Paul's Romans 7:9-25 wretched man with the biblical description of a spiritually healthy born-again Christian:

Paul's wretched man is brought death by God's commandment (Rom. 7:10). *However, the born-again Christian* not only loves to obey Jesus, but he or she finds life in Jesus' commandments, and that life is life to the full (John 6:68, 10:10, 14:21).

Paul's wretched man is unspiritual (Rom. 7:14). *However, the born-again Christian* is indeed spiritual, for he has been born of the Spirit, is part of a spiritual house designed to offer spiritual sacrifices to God and lives by and keeps in step with the Holy Spirit (John 3:7-8, 1 Pet. 4 2:5 and Gal. 5:24-25).

Paul's wretched man is sold as a slave to sin (Rom. 7:14). *However, the born-again Christian* is no longer a slave to sin, for he has been freed from sin's bondage by the power of the Holy Spirit and the blood of Jesus (Rom. 6:14, 17, 18 and 22).

Paul's wretched man Has sin living in him (Rom. 7:17). *However, the born-again Christian* has the Holy Spirit and Jesus Christ living in him (1 Cor. 3:16; Col. 1:27).

Paul's wretched man is controlled by sin (Rom. 7:17-18). *However, the born-again Christian* is not controlled by the sinful nature, but by the Holy Spirit (Rom. 6:6, 8:9; 1 Cor. 3:16).

Paul's wretched man has nothing good living in him (Rom. 7:18). *However, the born-again Christian* has God living in him (Gal. 2:20; 1 Cor. 3:16). It doesn't get any better than that!

Paul's wretched man finds it impossible to do good (Rom. 7:18). *However, the born-again Christian* is created in Christ Jesus to do good works and can do all things through Him who gives the strength (Eph. 2:10; Phil. 4:13).

Paul's wretched man is a prisoner of the law of sin and death (Rom. 7:23). *However, the born-again Christian* has been set free from all kinds of bondage by Jesus Himself (John 8:36).

Paul's wretched man is a slave to sin because he is still living according to the sinful nature (Rom. 7:25). *However, the born-again Christian* is no longer a slave to sin for Jesus has set him free from sin's power and control (Rom. 6:1-2, 6, 14, 18, 22).

Paul's wretched man is a wretched man indeed (v. 24). *However, the born-again Christian* is totally blessed, for God has blessed him with every spiritual blessing in Christ Jesus (Eph. 1:3).

The above should be enough to see the difference between Paul's wretched man and what God has created His children in Christ to be. Why then are so many Christians living wretched, defeated lives? Why do some Christians find themselves unable to do the good they want to do, as with Paul's wretched man?

> Gal 5:16-17
> 16 So I say, **live by the Spirit, and you will not gratify the desires of the sinful nature.**
> 17 For **the sinful nature desires what is contrary to the Spirit,** and the Spirit what is contrary to the sinful nature. They are in conflict with each other, **so that you do not do what you want.**

According to the above passage, Christians who fail to live as they should are doing so simply because they are living according to the sinful nature rather than by the Holy Spirit.

Paul's Wretched Man

Living according to the sinful nature is not God's plan for those who have been purchased by the blood of Jesus. God's plan for His children is to make them new creations in Christ who are living wonderful, joy-filled, Spirit-led lives (Gal. 5:22-25). Living according to the sinful nature always results in spiritual death:

> Rom. 8:13-14
> 13 For **if you live according to the sinful nature, you will die**; but if by the Spirit you put to death the misdeeds of the body, you will live,
> 14 because **those who are led by the Spirit of God are sons of God.**

Wow! God not only tells us that those who live according to the sinful nature will die (spiritually), but that **"those who are led by the Spirit of God are sons of God."** God loves you incredibly, and He wants to fill you with His Spirit and set you free from all destructive influences in your life.

It is not the norm for the "sons of God" to be sold as slaves to sin. And it is unthinkable that those who are led by the Holy Spirit would be unable to do the good they want to do, as it is with Paul's wretched man.

The glorious good news is that God not only sent Jesus so that our sins could be forgiven, but also to set us free from the control of the sinful nature:

> Rom. 8:3-4
> 3 For **what the law was powerless to do in that it was weakened by the sinful nature, <u>God did</u> by sending his own Son** in the likeness of sinful man **to be a sin offering**. And so he condemned sin in sinful man,
> 4 in order that the righteous requirements of the law might be fully met in us, who **do not live according to the sinful nature but according to the Spirit.**

Dear Christians, it is extremely important that you see that Paul's description of the wretched man was written solely to give us a picture of what it is like to live under the law and/or to be under the control of the sinful nature. This same Paul who said, "What a wretched man I am. Who shall rescue me from this body of death?" answered this question in the next verse and again three verses later by saying, "…through Christ Jesus, the law of the Spirit of life set me free from the law of sin and death" (Rom. 8:2). Jesus had set him free from that wretched life, and he who the Son sets free is free indeed!

People will live according to what they believe. If Christians believe it is normal to live under the control of the sinful nature that is how they will live. They will never have the faith to grasp how awesome the power of the indwelling Holy Spirit is and how completely Jesus has saved us from sin and its control.

I am not saying that Christians never sin, but I am saying that it is abnormal, and unscriptural, for Christians to live under the power and control of sin, as it is with Paul's wretched man. We all sin, but those who belong to Jesus can, with God's help, overcome any sin they have been in bondage to as they walk in the glorious power of the Holy Spirit (Rom. 6:2, 6, 12-14, 22; Gal. 5:16; Phil. 4:13; 1 John 3:6-10).

I cannot imagine how any true Christian can live like Paul's wretched man and still be an effective witness for the life and power of Jesus. Can you imagine witnessing to someone and asking, "Wouldn't you like to become a Christian so you can be a wretched person like me?" I would much rather be able to say, "Come to and trust in Jesus. He will fill you with His love and power and set you free from all spiritual bondage. He will also give you a new life of peace, love and joy that will blow your mind! He did it for me, and He will do it for you!"

God, in His infinite love, grace and wisdom has predestined us to be conformed to the likeness of His Son (Rom. 8:29), not to the likeness of Paul's wretched man. Thank God that our Savior and Master is a "way-maker" and a "life-changer!"

CHAPTER 8

Predestination – Clearing Up the Confusion

Predestination is about as easy to understand for many Christians as Einstein's Theory of Relativity. His theory is thoroughly foreign to non-geniuses like me. But what about the topic of predestination? Is it really all that complicated? Does God really put topics in the Bible just to confuse us? No!

In order to understand what the Bible says about predestination and why it is so confusing to many Christians, let's start off with a little history on the main source of the confusion…five-point Calvinism.

Augustine introduced his teaching on predestination, an important element of Calvinism, late in the fourth or early in the fifth century. He taught that Jesus did not die for all people, but only for those God had chosen and predestined to be His children. All others were predestined to go to hell. It was not until hundreds of years later that John Calvin revived and expanded on this doctrine.

Arminianism, which is basically the opposite of Calvinism, advocates that a Christian can forfeit his or her salvation by turning from Christ. However, our focus should not be on the teachings of either of these "isms," but on what the Bible actually says. It is sad that Christians side with or identify themselves with either of these "isms," as doing so causes division and takes the focus off Jesus. I don't want to be known as a Calvinist or as an Armenian, but as a Bible-believing, Jesus-loving Christian.

The extreme position held by true Calvinists is that predestination is the divine foreordaining of all that happens, including the salvation of some and eternal destruction of others. In other words, a true Calvinist believes that God elects some to salvation and others to damnation with no regard to their personal choices or anything they would do or not do.

Calvinism also teaches that salvation is solely dependent on God's sovereign will, which no one can resist. Those who are chosen for salvation must, in God's time, come to a saving faith in Jesus. Your will has nothing to do with it. Simply put, Calvinism teaches that God creates and chooses some for salvation and others for eternal damnation.

The Extreme of True Calvinism – "Five Point Calvinism"
(Otherwise Known as T.U.L.I.P.)

Let's explain the Calvinist's "T.U.L.I.P." doctrine. Here is what each letter represents:

Total Depravity
Unconditional Election
Limited Atonement (also known as Particular Atonement)
Irresistible Grace
Perseverance of the Saints (also known as "Once Saved, Always Saved")

Total Depravity: This point asserts that all humans are completely depraved and unable to even desire God of their own free will. Man has no ability to choose between good and evil, nor can he choose to repent.

Being that all humans are totally depraved, they are also unable to choose good without God's intervention. Therefore, it is God who chooses who will be saved and who will not. Our life, character or choices have nothing to do with God's decisions. Those God has chosen, He also causes to receive

Jesus, predestining them for eternal life. All others shall perish. Therefore, each individual's destination is solely based on God's desire and not on anything we choose or do.

<u>My comments</u>: Although those who believe the above use certain scriptures to make their point, their conclusions cannot be found anywhere in the Bible. They also ignore a great part of God's Word that would temper their belief and bring them to a more biblical conclusion.

If it were true that God chooses who will be saved and who will not, based solely on His desires, everyone would be saved, for the Bible tells us that God is "not wanting **anyone** to perish, but **everyone** to come to repentance" (2 Peter 3:9; 1 Tim. 2:3-4). However, not everyone is saved, because everyone has a free will and can choose to receive or reject Jesus as they please.

If God created man with no ability to repent, it would not only be unjust, but it would be sinister for God to "command all people everywhere to repent" (Acts 17:30), and then send them to hell for failing to do that which God gave them no ability to do. That would be like commanding an armless man to row the boat and then throwing him overboard for failing to do so.

Also, how could Joshua command Israel to "Choose for yourselves this day whom you will serve…" (Josh. 24:15), if it were not possible for them to choose for or against God? And why would Jesus tell Jerusalem, "…how I longed to gather your children [the Jews] together, as a hen gathers her chicks under her wings, but you were not willing," if their own will was not what determined their acceptance or rejection of Him? Jesus attributed the lost condition of these Jews to their own unwillingness, not to the lack of God's election.

The whole argument that man's depravity includes his inability to choose between good and bad is foolish. Although all are unrighteous outside of Jesus, whoever wills can, with the help of the Holy Spirit, receive Him as Lord and Savior, escape the corruption of this world and enter into the eternal life that is found only in Jesus.

Unconditional **Election**: Calvinism teaches that God does not base His choice (election) about who will go to heaven or hell on anything He sees in an individual or any choice an individual makes. God chooses those who will be saved and then causes them to receive Jesus. God then predestines those He causes to receive Jesus to eternal life and the rest to perish.

My comments: Please see "Biblical Predestination - Simple and to the Point" (page 67) for a more detailed explanation of how God's choices are based on His foreknowledge (Rom. 8:29-30). God does not choose some and condemn others indiscriminately or without reason. Just and true are His ways (Rev. 15:3)!

Limited **Atonement**: Calvinism teaches that Jesus died only for the elect…those who God has chosen and predestined for salvation. Although Jesus' sacrifice was sufficient for all, it is not "effective" for all. The atonement is only effective for those God has chosen and all others will end up in hell.

My comments: The Bible clearly states that "Christ died for sins once for all, the righteous for the unrighteous, to bring you to God" (1 Peter 3:18). The atonement is for all and not just for a limited number of people. The idea that Jesus' death is not effective for some, simply because God wanted it that way, is foreign to the Bible.

We find the word "whoever" in the Bible more times than I care to count. God offers salvation to whoever will come to Jesus. Jesus said, "For God so loved the world that He gave His one and only Son, that **whoever** believes in Him shall not perish but have eternal life" (John 3:16).

Predestination – Clearing Up the Confusion

God "so loved the world," not just a chosen few. And "whoever" believes in Jesus shall not perish, not just a chosen few. It is hard for me to imagine that some actually believe that our God, who is love and loves all, would turn around and have Jesus die for some, and then deny the power of His sacrifice to multitudes of others. God does not create people for the sole purpose of sending them to hell.

Irresistible Grace: Calvinism teaches that when God calls those He has predestined (the elect) to Jesus, He makes it impossible for them to resist His offer of salvation.

This doctrine also teaches that God gives two types of calls. There is an "external call," which is God's offer of salvation to everyone, and then there is an "internal call," which God gives only to His elect. This "internal call" is irresistible and it is by grace. That is why it is called "irresistible grace."

The "irresistible grace" doctrine also teaches that the Holy Spirit causes those who receive God's "internal call" to willingly and freely repent of their sinful ways and receive Jesus as their Lord and Savior. Those to whom God chooses not to give this "internal call" cannot possibly respond to God's offer of salvation and, as a result, they will perish.

<u>My comments</u>: It amazes me that anyone would believe that our loving God, who "is not wanting any to perish, but everyone to come to repentance" (2 Pet. 3:9), would actually offer everyone salvation, but then deny multitudes the ability to repent and receive Jesus for the salvation of their souls. That would be equivalent to offering a litter of puppies food they direly need, then duct-taping their mouths so that they cannot possibly eat it.

The doctrine of irresistible grace consists of a series of contradictions. First it tells us that God offers salvation to all, but then it says He only allows some to be saved by it. It also says that God gives an "external call" to all, including those who cannot possibly respond to it.

Why would God call people He has already predetermined cannot come? And where is this "external" and "internal" call ever mentioned in the Bible?

Also, if God "is not wanting any to perish, but all to come to repentance," why doesn't He just give this irresistible "internal call" to everyone so that no one would perish? How cruel it would be for God to send people to hell after making it impossible for them to come to Jesus and be saved.

The teaching of "irresistible grace" is another Calvinistic teaching that cannot be found anywhere in the Bible. God does not force anyone to choose or reject Him. In His great wisdom God has given us a free will to choose or reject His plan for our lives as we please.

This teaching also tells us that God causes this "internal call" to be irresistible, but then says that those who receive it (His elect) "willingly and freely come to God." How can a person willingly and freely do something God has made impossible for him or her to resist? There is nothing free about doing what someone else makes you do. Their response to this "irresistible grace" could only be a robotic response to an irresistible force and could never be a love-response.

However, the Bible tells us that the grace of God is offered to all through the sacrifice and poured-out blood of Jesus Christ. The cross is a demonstration of God's limitless love for all, not for just a chosen few (Rom. 5:8). All who choose Jesus will have life, and all who reject Jesus will experience eternal destruction. Again, the doctrine of irresistible grace is just another harmful, man-made Calvinistic doctrine.

Perseverance of the Saints ("Once Saved, Always Saved"): This point asserts that those God has chosen and predestined cannot lose or forfeit their salvation. Even if they fall away, they will always repent and return to the Lord. Otherwise, they were never really saved in the first place.

My comments: This whole book addresses the once saved, always saved doctrine, so I will not say much about it here. However, I would like to comment on the often-referred-to idea that "if one falls away or is living in sin and does not return to the Lord, he or she was never saved in the first place." I know some very good, sincere Christians who believe this. However, that does not change the fact that this teaching cannot be substantiated by any verse or passage in the Bible and, therefore, is totally unbiblical and should be rejected as such (see page 153 for more on this subject).

It is important to see that not all who believe once saved, always saved subscribe to "five point Calvinism," nor do they accept all of John Calvin's teaching on predestination. Most who believe once saved, always saved will subscribe to certain parts of it and reject others.

Biblical Predestination - Simple and to the Point

According to the Bible, God does predestine people to certain eternal destinations. However, it is important to see that He never does so haphazardly, but according to His foreknowledge of what they will choose and do of their own free will:

Rom. 8:29-30
29 For **those God foreknew he also predestined** to be conformed to the likeness of his Son, that he might be the firstborn among many brothers.
30 And **those he predestined,** he also called; those he called, he also justified; those he justified, he also glorified.

<u>A Biblical Definition of Predestination</u>: God determining your destiny based on what He foreknew about your life and what you would or would not do of your own free will.

Let's say I had a group of students and I would that none would fail, but that all would pass, just as God would that none would perish, but that all would come to repentance and be saved (2 Peter 3:9).

Now let's also suppose I had a projector that could miraculously project the future. I could simply turn it on, type in a name and view how each student would do in class as a result of their own choices and free will. And then, by this foreknowledge, I could determine in advance (predestine) their destiny...who would pass and who would fail. I would not be interfering with their will and choices in the slightest. I would just determine their grade ahead of time, based on what I foreknew of them, just as God determines our destiny ahead of time, based on what He foreknows of us.

God is God. And, as God, He is not only omnipotent (all-powerful) and omnipresent (all-present), but He is also omniscient (all-knowing). He knows the past, present and future all at one time. Therefore He cannot help but know the choices any given person will make in the future, even one hundred or one thousand years from now.

Let's look at it like this: We see the parade of life going by as from the street curb; therefore, we see it going by one part at a time. We can only see what is presently there and sometimes remember that which has passed. However, we do not know what is coming around the corner, for we cannot see the future.

But God sees the parade of our lives from a whole different perspective. He sees the parade as though viewing it from the highest building...from start to finish, all at the same time from an eternal vantage point. God knows everything we will say and do before we say or do it. He can determine our final destination based on what He foreknows we will choose throughout our life of our own free will. Therefore, "those

God foreknew, he also predestined." And so, biblical predestination does not interfere with one's free will in the slightest.

> 1 Peter 1:1-2
> 1 Peter, an apostle of Jesus Christ. **To God's elect,** strangers in the world, scattered throughout Pontus, Galatia, Cappadocia, Asia and Bithynia,
> 2 **who have been chosen <u>according to the foreknowledge</u> of God the Father,** through the sanctifying work of the Spirit, for obedience to Jesus Christ and sprinkling by his blood: Grace and peace be yours in abundance.

We see, in the above verses, that there is such a thing as "God's elect." However, we also see that God's elect have been chosen for salvation based on "the foreknowledge of God the Father." God predestines to eternal life those He foreknew would receive and follow Jesus (Rom. 8:29; 1 Pet. 1:1-2), and then He calls them His "elect."

God offers salvation to all, but only those who receive and follow Jesus as their Lord and Savior will possess it. Therefore, each person chooses heaven or hell by choosing to receive or reject Jesus. And so God also predestines those he foreknew would choose to reject or abandon Jesus to eternal damnation.

The idea that God would actually create certain people just to send them to hell, without giving them a choice in the matter, should be totally rejected. Again, the Bible tells us:

> 2 Peter 3:9
> The Lord is not slow in keeping his promise, as some understand slowness. He is patient with you, **not wanting anyone to perish, but everyone to come to repentance.**

God will not force anyone to receive Jesus as Lord and Savior…He will not force anyone to believe one way or the other. Instead, He draws people to His Son by the love He demonstrated for us on the cross (Rom. 5:8). He offers salvation to all through Christ Jesus, but then we must choose to receive or reject His gracious offer.

<u>"You Did Not Choose Me, But I Chose You..."</u>

Some who believe once saved, always saved may ask, "What about John 15:16? It tells us that God does choose some to be saved and others not to be saved."

> John 15:16
> **You did not choose me, but I chose you** and appointed you to go and bear fruit — fruit that will last. Then the Father will give you whatever you ask in my name.

In the above verse, Jesus is speaking to His Apostles. In context, Jesus is simply telling them that He chose them and not vice versa. He found them busy with their various employments and told them to follow Him.

When I was a youngster, my friends and I would gather to play baseball or football. Two boys were then chosen to be captains, and then each would pick who they wanted on their team. That process did not interfere with anyone's free will in the slightest. As a matter of fact I could say, "No way, I'm not going to be on your team," any time I wanted to.

When Jesus chose His team (the twelve Apostles), He chose them based on what He knew of them and on what He foreknew they would do in the future. All they had to do was respond to His call and say, "Yes, Lord, I will follow you." Of course Jesus foreknew that Judas would not continue to follow Him, but would be used to fulfill God's plan of redemption by the cross.

Being that Jesus was talking about choosing His Apostles, the above verse should not be taken out of context to say that

Predestination – Clearing Up the Confusion

God creates and chooses some for salvation and others for destruction...which brings us to the next question.

Does God Choose Some to Be Saved and Others to Be Lost?

Some who believe once saved, always saved refer to Romans 9:11-22 to say that God chooses some to be saved and others to be lost...and that He does so without any consideration of what they would do or the kind of person each would be.

This passage definitely needs to be addressed in light of other scriptures. Therefore, as we get into this passage, let's be sure to keep the formula for solid biblical interpretation in mind:

Formula for solid biblical interpretation:

Passage "A" + Passage "B" = Truth (Even if it does not seem to make sense to you)

And we should avoid the formula for biblical distortion:

Formula for biblical distortion:

Passage "A" + "My preconceived belief" = Passage "B" cannot mean what it clearly says

Following the formula for solid biblical interpretation, we will examine Romans 9:11-22 along with what God says about man's responsibility. Our purpose is to see if the Bible really says that God chooses some to be saved and others to be lost, without any consideration of their character, actions and choices.

Leading up to the following passage, Paul has been talking about the fact that not all natural Israelites are the children of promise (see Rom. 9:6-7). And so, although both of Rebecca's children had the same father, God chose one to be the ancestor of the Messiah and the other not to be. This choice was based solely on His decision and not on anything either child had done. Let's go through this passage one or two verses at a time:

> Rom. 9:11-22
> 11 Yet, **before the twins were born or had done anything good or bad** — in order that God's purpose in election might stand:
> 12 not by works but by him who calls — she was told, **"The older will serve the younger."**

God had chosen Jacob to be the ancestor of the Messiah and the recipient of the promises. This choice was not based on anything Jacob had done, but on the basis of God's sovereign will. And who can argue with God? So He simply says:

> 13 Just as it is written: **"Jacob I loved, but Esau I hated."**

In other words, God rejected Esau and chose Jacob to be the heir of His promises.

> 14 What then shall we say? **Is God unjust? Not at all!**
> 15 For he says to Moses, **"I will have mercy on whom I have mercy, and I will have compassion on whom I have compassion."**

God makes it clear that we have no right to judge or criticize Him for His sovereign decisions. Every decision God makes is based on His infinite love, mercy, wisdom and foreknowledge; therefore, they are never unjust.

> 16 **It does not, therefore, depend on man's desire or effort, but on God's mercy.**

Most who cling to a Calvinistic view of predestination take the "it" in this verse to mean salvation. However, the "it" in this verse is talking about God's sovereign choice to do with and use whoever He wants in whatever way He pleases. It says nothing about salvation. Paul then uses the Pharaoh of Egypt as an example to make this point:

> 17 For the Scripture says to Pharaoh: **"I raised you up for this very purpose, that I might display my power in you and that my name might be proclaimed in all the earth."**

God chose to use Pharaoh for His own glory. We must remember that God foreknew Pharaoh's heart before he was born and, therefore, God's choice to do what He did with Pharaoh was also based on His foreknowledge of Pharaoh's stubborn character. As a result, no one can say that God was unjust in His decision to use Pharaoh as He did.

> 18 Therefore **God has mercy on whom he wants to have mercy,** and **he hardens whom he wants to harden.**

This is no doubt a reference to the hardening of Pharaoh's heart. But why did God choose to harden Pharaoh's heart? Was it without reason? Did our loving and just God harden Pharaoh's heart unjustly? Not at all! That would be contrary to His divine character.

It was not until Pharaoh had already hardened his own heart against the Lord (Exodus 8:15, 32) that the Lord said (in so many words), "Okay, if that's the way you want it, I will harden your heart permanently." God simply established the hardened heart Pharaoh already had.

> 19 One of you will say to me: "Then why does God still blame us? For who resists his will?"
> 20 But who are you, O man, to talk back to God? "Shall what is formed say to him who formed it, 'Why did you make me like this?'"

73

21 Does not the potter have the right to make out of the same lump of clay some pottery for noble purposes and some for common use?
22 What if God, choosing to show his wrath and make his power known, bore with great patience the objects of his wrath — prepared for destruction?

The above is a reference to God's sovereignty. The point of verses 20-22 is that we have no right to question God's decisions. He can do whatever He pleases to and with whom He pleases. But, again, we must remember that God does what He pleases based on His infinite love, just character and divine foreknowledge of each person.

No one should ever say the above verses mean that God chooses and prepares some for salvation and others for destruction without a just basis for His decisions. Again, God is **"not wanting <u>anyone</u> to perish, but everyone to come to repentance"** (2 Peter 3:9). Therefore, if it were not for each individual's freedom to receive or reject Jesus, all would be saved according to God's great desire.

God will never force anyone to receive and follow Jesus. As a result, there are those who will never choose Jesus and there are those who will. There are also those who will receive Him, and then choose to "turn away from the faith" at the expense of their salvation (Matt. 24:10-13).

God predestines those He foreknew would follow Jesus to eternal life and those He foreknew would reject Jesus to eternal damnation. And God wants those who follow Him to do so because they love Him, not because they are robots without a heart and will of their own.

Understanding how God's foreknowledge works together with predestination is extremely important. However, there is another important topic that is critical for an accurate and biblical understanding of the security of the believer…the three stages of the Christian life. Although these stages are seldom taught, they are clearly demonstrated in the Bible.

CHAPTER 9

The Three Stages of the Christian Life

Life is a journey that consists of various stages. We all start off by being born, then we go through the infant stage, the toddler stage, the "youngster" stage, etc. At 70 years old, I am presently in the over-the-hill stage and believe me, once you get over the hill life picks up speed as you head toward the end of your life on this earth. But that's okay; Jesus is waiting there to sweep us up to heaven.

The Christian experience is also a journey that consists of various stages. Biblically speaking, there are three distinct stages from start to finish:

1. Coming to Jesus and being born again (initial salvation)
2. Our journey on earth (life between initial and final salvation)
3. The Christian's final arrival and eternity in heaven (final salvation)

Okay, okay…I can't blame you for thinking, "Now wait a minute. Does the Bible really demonstrate that the Christian life actually consists of the three stages mentioned above?" Well, let's dig in and find out.

Stage One of the Christian Life – Coming to Jesus and Being Born Again

The initial stage of salvation is the born-again stage (John 3:3), which is the result of believing, repenting and receiving. We are saved immediately when we truly repent of our sinful direction in life and receive Jesus as our Lord and Savior:

> Acts 3:19 [Peter preaching]
> **Repent, then, and turn to God, so that your sins may be wiped out**, that times of refreshing may come from the Lord,

> John 1:12
> Yet **to all who received him**, to those **who believed** in his name, **he gave the right to become children of God**--

I'm not going to elaborate on this, for every true Christian knows we must believe in and receive Jesus as our Lord and Savior to be saved. However, coming to and receiving Jesus is just the beginning of the Christian experience. We have gained access into this grace through faith, but we still must live out our Christianity:

> Rom. 5:1-2
> 1 Therefore, since we have been justified through faith, we have peace with God **through our Lord Jesus Christ**,
> 2 through whom <u>**we have gained access by faith**</u> **into this grace in which we <u>now stand</u>**. And we rejoice in the hope of the glory of God.

So the Bible makes it clear that once we have gained access by faith into this grace we must then "stand" as we live out the Christian life, which brings us to stage two:

<u>Stage Two of the Christian Life - Our Journey on Earth</u>

The Three Stages of the Christian Life

Wouldn't it be nice if when we received the Lord we were immediately transferred into heaven? Just think...there would be no trials, heartaches or temptations to deal with. However, there also would be no spiritual growth, which comes as a result of the trials we go through on this earth (1 Peter 1:6-7). And if all Christians were taken into heaven as soon as they were saved, who would have been here to lead us to Jesus?

Well, being that going directly to heaven after being born again will not work, we have to stick around here and live out the Christian life until God decides to take us home. So stage two of the Christian journey is the live-the-Christian-life stage. It is where we are right now, and God does not leave us without instructions on how to live this life:

1 Peter 2:11
Dear friends, I urge you, **as aliens and strangers in the world, to abstain from sinful desires, which war against your soul**.

In the above verse, Peter instructs us to abstain from sinful desires, which war against our souls. The Christian life is incredibly wonderful, but it is also a time of spiritual warfare. And I assure you that the only way to win this battle is to be yielded to and led by the Holy Spirit:

Rom. 8:13-14
13 For **if you live according to the sinful nature, you will die**; but if **by the Spirit you put to death the misdeeds of the body, you will live,**
14 because **those who are led by the Spirit of God are sons of God.**

One of the enemies we must fight against in this life is the sinful nature. The sinful nature is that part of us that has a bent towards sin. Whether we want to or not, we must fight this fight or, according to the above verses, we will die. Of course, Paul was speaking of spiritual death. The battle against the sinful nature is a matter of spiritual life or death. And who will win this battle? That depends on who or what your heart truly belongs to.

You can be sure of victory if you have submitted yourself to Jesus and are filled with and led by the Holy Spirit. The Holy Spirit is God living in you, and no one is greater than God. It is only by the Holy Spirit that you can put to death the misdeeds of the body (Rom. 8:13).

The subject of the sinful nature is huge, so all I am going to say here is that the sinful nature is bad to the bone, and you cannot improve it. The best thing you can do is to crucify it by living in obedience to the Holy Spirit (Gal. 5:24-25).

The sinful nature is not the only enemy we must fight against during this stage of the Christian life. There is another enemy who is constantly looking for ways to destroy us:

1 Peter 5:8-9
8 Be self-controlled and alert. **Your enemy the devil** prowls around like a roaring lion **looking for someone to devour.**
9 Resist him, standing firm in the faith, because you know that your brothers throughout the world are undergoing the same kind of sufferings.

In the second stage of the Christian life, we are also involved in a spiritual battle against the devil himself…a battle in which the Spirit-empowered, Spirit-led Christian is sure to have victory. However, those who love themselves, this world and sin more than Jesus are sure to lose this battle, which will result in disaster. And so the Holy Spirit instructs:

1 Tim. 6:12
Fight the good fight of the faith. **Take hold of the eternal life** to which you were called **when you made your good confession** in the presence of many witnesses.

In the verse above, God tells us to take hold of something. If I threw you a rope and told you to take hold of it, it would be clear that you had not yet taken hold of it. It would be pretty stupid of me to tell you to take hold of something you already held in your hand.

Hmmm. Let's think about this. Paul tells Timothy to take hold of the eternal life to which he was called. In other words, Timothy, who was already saved, had not yet taken hold of the eternal life Paul was talking about. What can this mean? If we have eternal life, but are told to take hold of eternal life, is there actually a phase of eternal life we do not yet possess…one we must take hold of?

> Mark 10:29-30
> 29 "I tell you the truth," Jesus replied, "**no one who has left home or brothers or sisters or mother or father or children or fields for me and the gospel 30 will fail to receive** a hundred times as much in this present age (homes, brothers, sisters, mothers, children and fields — and with them, persecutions) **and in the age to come, eternal life.**"

And so there is a stage of eternal life that we do not yet have…a stage we will experience in "the age to come."

In the following verses, Paul is speaking to those who are still in stage two of the Christian journey, but are drawing nearer to their final stage of salvation than when they first believed:

> Rom. 13:11-12
> 11 And do this, understanding the present time. The hour has come for you to wake up from your slumber, because **our salvation is nearer now than when we first believed.**

12 The night is nearly over; the day is almost here. So let us put aside the deeds of darkness and put on the armor of light.

Paul encouraged these Christians to wake up spiritually, because their salvation was nearer than when they first believed. Paul is writing to people who already had salvation, but reminded them that they were drawing nearer to some sort, or phase, of salvation that was in the future.

The above scriptures can only make sense if there are stages to salvation. They were already saved, but stage three of their salvation, which is being with Jesus in heaven, was drawing closer. They would soon be with Jesus forever, which brings us to the final stage of the Christian journey:

Stage Three of the Christian Life – Arriving and Spending Eternity in Heaven

Stage three is the final stage of the Christian Journey. The term "final salvation" is being used to describe the eternal life that those who stand firm to the end will receive in what Jesus called the age to come (Matt. 24:10-13; Mark 10:30).

When those who believe once saved, always saved say we have eternal life as soon as we receive Jesus as Lord and Savior, they are correct. However, many fail to see that receiving Jesus is only the beginning, and that eternal life in the age to come is only for those who remain in Jesus to the end (Matt. 24:10-13).

We have not yet arrived in heaven. We are still awaiting the eternal life that is in the age to come, so Jude says:

Jude 21
Keep yourselves in God's love **as you wait for the mercy of our Lord Jesus Christ** <u>to bring you to eternal life</u>.

In the above verse, Jude is speaking to "…those who are loved by God the Father and kept by Jesus Christ" (Jude 1). So

Jude is clearly speaking to people who are already saved, but are still waiting for the mercy of Jesus Christ to bring them eternal life. And what else can this eternal life be, but the eternal life we are to receive in the age to come (Mark 10:30)?

Biblical salvation can be likened to having your eternal cruise ticket paid for by Jesus, but then you must cross this sea of life until you reach your final destination, which is heaven. You have the time of boarding the ship of salvation (initial salvation and eternal life), the trip across the ocean of life (present salvation and eternal life) and your final arrival to heaven's port and eternal safety (final salvation and eternal life).

If you have received Jesus as your Lord and Savior, you are presently on board the Jesus-ship and are traveling toward the shores of heaven. However, Jesus made it clear in John 15:1-6 that you must remain in Him (on board His ship) in order to reach your final destination in heaven. And what of those who do not? What of those who abandon the Jesus-ship to swim their life away in the sea of sin?

Some people think it is impossible for Christians to end up being lost by abandoning Jesus. However, the Bible tells us that it is absolutely possible, and I know some people who have done just that. I have no doubt that these people knew Jesus before abandoning the faith. They openly expressed their love for Him, they were faithful in devotions, and they had even won people to the Lord who are still following Jesus today.

Those who jump ship to swim in the sea of sin will not experience final salvation. According to Gal. 5:16-21, they will lose out on the kingdom of God because of their own foolish choices...that is unless they get back on board before it's too late (repent).

Who Will Experience Final Salvation?

The above question is really asking, "Who will reach God's intended destination for those who receive Jesus?" Let's look at this another way.

The Gospel Truth

Back in the 1950's, my friends and I would occasionally take the Greyhound Bus to San Francisco from Pittsburg California, the town I grew up in. Once there, we would enjoy the day by taking the trolley to Golden Gate Park, go to the zoo, or maybe take a ride to Playland at the Beach. That's right, right across from the beach, San Francisco once had an amusement park with a funhouse, roller coaster, Ferris wheel, bumper cars, alpine racer, tilt-a-whirl, crazy-daisy, and a bunch of other fun stuff.

Needless to say, when we got on that bus, we were excited. We knew we were going to have a great time after arriving in San Francisco. However, not everyone who got on the bus stayed on the bus. Because of various desires and priorities, people got off the bus at various points before it reached the end of the line. Those who did not stay on the bus to the end did not arrive at our final, and totally enjoyable, destination.

This is a common-sense story with a very biblical application. This story applies perfectly to the Christian's journey of life and his or her final destination in heaven. Jesus said:

> Matt. 24:13
> 12 Because of the increase of wickedness, the love of most will grow cold,
> **13 but he who stands firm <u>to the end</u> will be saved**.

Who does Jesus say will be saved? Christians who began in the faith and have since turned away from the faith? No way! How about those who had once received the grace of God, but have since fallen from grace? Not at all!

Jesus declared that he who stands firm to the end will be saved. Not all who begin the Christian journey of life will reach final salvation. God's Word makes it clear that those who abandon Jesus before reaching heaven just aren't going to make it. To say that a person who has been saved, but has since abandoned Jesus will still reach his eternal destination in heaven is contrary to what the Bible clearly teaches.

At a very young age, I was taught that if anything is worth doing at all, it is worth doing right. And along with that teaching was, "If you start something, finish it...otherwise you are wasting your time." These are words of wisdom. After all, it is not the person who boards the bus that will reach his destination, but the person who remains on the bus till the end of the journey.

In this book, I go into great detail to share what God's word really says about the Once Saved, Always Saved doctrine as opposed to the doctrine of Conditional Security. However, focusing on these doctrines without explaining the entire gospel can lead to some misunderstanding. So, in the next chapter, you will find the entire gospel in a nutshell...a panoramic view of the gospel that many have never seen.

CHAPTER 10

The Entire Gospel in a Nutshell

Ahhh, I had finally finished this book…so I thought. While in church today, the Lord began to speak to me about injecting one more chapter into this book. Why? Because this book focuses on the doctrines of Unconditional Security (Once Saved, Always Saved) as opposed to Conditional Security (Salvation can be lost) rather than the entire gospel message.

Focusing on these two doctrines without an explanation of the entire gospel can lead to some misunderstanding. Therefore, it is important that I clarify what I believe concerning God's great message of salvation in order to avoid being misunderstood or misrepresented. Thus, in this chapter, I present the entire gospel, along with it's supporting doctrines, in a nutshell.

The word "gospel" simply means "good news." So let's see what's so good about the "good news" handed down to us by the Holy Spirit through the Apostles:

1. The good news starts off with the fact that everyone on the face of this earth has sinned and needs to be saved.

Being that all have sinned, all must pay the price, or receive the wages, for their sin. The Bible tells us that the wages of sin is death (Rom. 3:23, 6:23). The word "death" means separation. Therefore, the penalty of sin is eternal separation from God in a state of perpetual suffering (Matt. 22:13, 25:30; 2 Peter 2:17; Jude 13).

It is this eternal penalty, among other harmful things, that we all need to be saved from. And the only way to be saved from this penalty is for someone who has never sinned to die for our sins in our place.

2. To understand the good news, we must understand that we cannot save ourselves.

Before coming to Jesus, we all were "dead in our transgressions" and were "by nature objects of God's wrath" (Eph. 2:1-3). In this state there is no way we could save ourselves. We were like a drowning man who is totally exhausted and powerless to save himself. Unless someone else pulls him out of the water, he will die.

In the same way, it is impossible for sinners to pay for their own sins in order to escape sin's penalty. The good news is that Jesus is willing and able to pull us from the waters of sin and eternal destruction.

3. The good news is that God loves us so much that He sent His one and only Son, Jesus, to pay the price for our sins.

God loves us more than we can imagine. But God is also a God of justice. He cannot allow our sins to go unpunished. Therefore, God made a way to save us from the punishment we so deserve and to maintain justice at the same time. God sent His one and only Son to suffer and die for our sins in our place (John 3:16). This way justice could be satisfied and our sins could be paid for and forgiven at the same time.

Jesus' death on the cross is God's greatest demonstration of His love for us (Rom. 5:8). We did nothing to deserve this great act of love and, therefore, salvation is totally by grace (it's undeserved) and is available to <u>all</u> who trust in Jesus as their

The Entire Gospel in a Nutshell

personal Lord and Savior (Eph. 2:8-9). This is good news indeed!

4. The good news is that those who come to Jesus by faith are no longer under the control of Satan, the destroyer.

Not only did Jesus save us, but He purchased us with His own blood...we belong to Him. As blood-bought children of God, Jesus has also freed us from the power of Satan, enabling us to live for the honor and glory of God (Rom. 1:6; Eph. 2:1-5; 1 Peter 1:18-19; 1 Cor. 6:19-20).

5. The good news is that, as a result of His great sacrifice, Jesus is now the only way to the Father.

Because He loved us enough to die in our place, the Father has made Jesus the only way to Himself. Jesus said, "I am the Way" to the Father, not "a way." Therefore Jesus said, "No one comes to the Father except through me." (John 14:6).

The good news is that God has given us the Best and made the Best the only way to Himself. All other so called ways are dangerous and harmful and will not bring anyone to eternal life. Satan loves it when people try other ways...ways that he has devised to lead them astray and into the pit of destruction.

6. The good news is that the Father puts us in Christ Jesus when we receive Jesus and are saved.

Eph 2:6-7
6 And God raised us up with Christ and seated us with him in the heavenly realms **in Christ Jesus**,
7 in order that in the coming ages he might show the incomparable riches of his grace, expressed in his kindness to us **in Christ Jesus**.

Salvation is not in a church, denomination, philosophy or any such thing. Salvation is found only in Christ Jesus, therefore, we must be in Him to be saved. Those who are in Jesus are saved and those who are not in Jesus are not saved. Thank you, Father, for placing us in Christ Jesus at the moment of salvation!

7. The good news is that God has made Jesus to be the Christian's glorious dwelling place and Heaven's Treasure Chest.

God places those who receive Jesus in Jesus, who is the Christ. Only those who are "in Christ" can receive God's glorious riches (Col. 2:2-3; Phil. 4:19). Every good thing that God has for us, including salvation, can be found only "in Christ Jesus." As a result, these spiritual riches are only for those who are put into Jesus by the Father.

It is extremely important not to miss the words "in Christ" or "in Christ Jesus" when reading the Bible. The words "in Christ" are used 91 times in the New Testament and, therefore, must be very important.

A study of each verse that uses these words reveals that:

1. We are "alive to God in Christ Jesus" (Rom. 6:11).
2. "The gift of eternal life is in Christ" (Rom. 6:23).
3. There is "no condemnation for those who are in Christ Jesus" (Rom. 8:1).
4. The love of God is found "in Christ Jesus" (Rom. 8:39).
5. We are "sanctified in Christ Jesus" (1 Cor. 1:2).
6. God's grace is found "in Christ Jesus" (1 Cor. 1:4).
7. Hope is found "in Christ" (1 Cor. 15:19).
8. We are made alive "in Christ" (1 Cor. 15:22).
9. We are made new creations when placed "in Christ" (2 Cor. 5:17).
10. We receive spiritual blessings "in Christ" (Eph. 1:3).
11. Believers are included "in Christ" (Eph. 1:13).
12. We are seated in heavenly realms "in Christ" (Eph. 2:6).

13. We are forgiven by God "in Christ" (Eph. 4:32).
14. God's glorious riches are found "in Christ Jesus" (Phil. 4:19).
15. Only those who are saved can be "in Christ" (Col. 1:2).

Oh, and let us not forget 1 Corinthians 1:30:

1 Cor 1:30
It is because of him that you are **in Christ Jesus, who has become for us wisdom from God — that is, our righteousness, holiness and redemption.**

Wow! How awesome is that! Because we are in Jesus, He has become our righteousness, holiness and redemption. In other words, as we remain in Him, God looks at us and sees His righteousness and holiness, instead of our imperfections! What good news!

There are 75 more times "in Christ" is used in the New Testament, revealing how important it is to be in Him. It is indeed good news that we receive so much good from God when "in Christ Jesus." That is why, in this book, I have likened Jesus to a ship (the "Jesus Ship") that we must be in to get to heaven and to receive all of God's great spiritual blessings.

8. Four things must happen for the Father to place us in Christ Jesus. These four things often happen simultaneously:

<u>We must believe.</u>

Only those who have faith can be saved, for only those who believe that Jesus is God's chosen Lord and Savior will receive Him as such. It is through faith that we become a child of God (John 1:12). We are saved by grace, through faith (Eph. 2:8-9). However, it is possible to believe without being saved (James 2:19-20). That is why the Bible gives us three more events that must take place for salvation.

<u>We must repent.</u>

It is no coincidence that, in the Gospel of Matthew, the first thing John the Baptist (Matt. 3:1-2) and Jesus (Matt. 4:17) preached was to repent. And the first thing that Peter preached after receiving the baptism of the Holy Spirit was that those listening to him must repent (Acts 2:38) so that their "sins could be wiped out" (Acts 3:19).

Repentance means to make an about-face in your life...to have a change of mind and heart about the sinful direction you are going so that you can turn around and start living for Jesus. No one can follow Jesus as their Lord without first choosing to abandon their life of sin (Matt. 7:21). Repentance does not mean being perfect, but it does mean, with God's help, making every effort to avoid sin and to be what God wants you to be (Heb. 12:14; 2 Pet. 1:5-11).

There are many unsaved people who believe in Jesus yet refuse to repent. They simply love their life of sin more than Him, and they will not be saved until they respond to the Holy Spirit's promptings to repent.

<u>We must receive Jesus as our Lord and Savior.</u>

The Bible tells us that we must receive Jesus...all of Him...to become a child of God (John 1:12). We cannot receive the Savior part without receiving the Lord part, for Jesus is both Lord and Savior (2 Peter 3:18). Those who do not want to receive Jesus as their Lord have not come to a place of repentance, nor have they truly been born again.

<u>We must be born again.</u>

It seems strange when I hear someone ask, "Is he a born-again Christian?" It seems strange because Jesus said you "must be born again" to be a child of God (John 3:3-6). Therefore, there can be no other kind of real Christian.

Jesus said we must be born of the Spirit (John 3:5). Being born of the Spirit happens when you receive Jesus as your Lord and Savior. At that very moment, all your sins are washed away and the Holy Spirit comes to live in you, imparting new spiritual life.

When we are born again, God puts us in Christ Jesus as new creations. The Bible tells us that "If anyone is in Christ, he is a new creation, the old is gone and the new has come" (2 Cor. 5:17). God's ultimate goal is to transform His new creations into the likeness of Jesus as they surrender their lives to Him (Rom. 8:29).

When one is born again, the change of heart is instant, but the transition from our old self to becoming more like Jesus takes time (2 Cor. 3:18). The born-again person does not become sinless, but the sin cycle is broken for those who truly know Jesus (1 John 3:6). Born-again people are no longer "slaves to sin" (Rom. 6:6, 17, 20), for they are the children of God whom Jesus has set "free indeed" (John 8:36). This is good news!

9. The good news is that we cannot be saved by works, religion or doctrine.

If we could be saved by works, religion, or doctrine, we would never know if we had done enough works, practiced enough religion or known enough doctrine to pay for our sins. Being that we can never do enough to pay for our own sins, the result of trying to do so will end in eternal destruction.

However, Jesus did do enough. Only being in Him can protect us from the wrath of God that is coming upon those who reject Jesus (John 3:36).

Only those who have a personal relationship with Jesus Christ can have eternal life:

1 John 5:20
We know also that the Son of God has come and has given us understanding, so that we may **know him who is true**. And we are **in him who is true** — even in his Son Jesus Christ. **He is the true God and eternal life.**

Being that salvation comes by knowing the one "who is true," only those who know Jesus as their personal Lord and Savior can be "in him who is true." The good news is that you don't have to search any farther than Jesus to find eternal life, for "He is the true God and eternal life."

10. The good news is that eternal security is found only in Christ Jesus. All who are in Jesus can be sure they will be with God in heaven when they leave this earth.

God's guarantee of eternal life is only for those who are in Christ Jesus. That's why Jesus tells us that Christians who fail to remain in Him will be "cut off...thrown into the fire and burned" (John 15:1-6). I have dedicated all of chapter five to these verses. If you haven't already done so, I suggest you read this most revealing chapter, for it gives us the truth about eternal security right from the mouth of Jesus.

Willfully living in sin is not the same as stumbling, which is something we all do (James 3:2). However, one cannot live in willful sin and in Jesus at the same time, for Jesus is "the source of eternal salvation for all who obey Him" (Heb. 5:9). Jesus does not provide eternal salvation for those who choose to turn from Him to live in disobedience and sin. They have rejected the source of all that is good to embrace all that is bad.

Jesus Himself said it is possible for a branch that is in Him (Christian) to be cut off from Him, so it must be possible. It is sinful to knowingly contradict what Jesus clearly says. I tremble at the thought of it.

This book contains a multitude of passages that make it clear that it is possible for wayward Christians to forfeit their salvation. Turning from Jesus to a life of sin is a serious mistake and should not be taken lightly.

The good news is that God accepts us as we are, but loves us too much to leave us as we are. God has given all who love Jesus the power to overcome any destructive thing that comes between them and living for Him. We can, in time, have victory over whatever sin has held us in bondage as we surrender our lives to Jesus. There is victory in Jesus!

11. The good news is that once we are saved, God does not leave us to work out our salvation on our own. He gives us the Holy Spirit to empower and help us to live out the Christian life.

Those who are in Christ Jesus also have God living in them by the person of the Holy Spirit (1 Cor. 3:16). Jesus speaks to and guides us through the Holy Spirit, therefore we are never alone as we walk this earth for His glory (John 16:14-15).

The more we surrender ourselves to the leading of the Holy Spirit, the more He will guide and strengthen us (Gal. 5:25). Jesus breathed the Holy Spirit into His Apostles personally (John 20:22), then later told them to wait in Jerusalem for the baptism of the Holy Spirit (Acts 1:4-5). This meant more power to be His witnesses (Acts 1:8).

God has this same power available for all who would deny the sinful nature in pursuit of this wonderful life in the Spirit (Gal. 5:24 -25). What good news!

12. The good news is that God not only calls Christians to pursue holiness, but helps them to live holy lives.

At the very moment we receive Jesus as our Lord and Savior, God justifies us, making us righteous in His sight. This righteousness is a gift from God that we did nothing to deserve. We are also cleansed of <u>all</u> our sins and are given a brand new start in life. We are born again with a changed heart and a new start. God then calls us to live out the righteousness He has freely given us in practical ways (James 2:22-24).

Jesus has set those who love Him free from the control of sin (Rom. 6:6), and those who the Son sets free are free indeed (John 8:36)! When they do sin, they hate it, confess it, and repent of it, for this is the way of those who love Jesus. In time, they will overcome their sin by the power of the Holy Spirit.

The Bible tells us that God has given us everything we need for life and godliness (2 Peter 1:3). We must not forget that we have the God who created the universe living and working in us to make us more like Jesus (1 Cor. 3:16).

Nothing is too hard for God, but we must work together with Him by pursuing holiness. That's why God commands us to "make every effort…to be holy," while reminding us that "without holiness no one will see the Lord" (Heb. 12:14). If we pursue holiness, He will work it in us.

This does not mean we will ever be totally perfect and sinless on this earth. However, we will be perfect when we are with our Lord in heaven. When we see Him as He is, we will be as He is (1John 3:2). Oh, the marvelous grace of God!

13. The good news is that once a person is saved, all past sins are erased and forever forgiven. He has also provided forgiveness for sins committed after a person's initial cleansing.

The teaching, "Christ died for our sins: past, present and future" is true, but sometimes misused. Our past sins are indeed totally wiped out when we receive Jesus as our Lord and Savior. However, some go so far as to say that, after being saved, our present and future sins are also automatically forgiven without having to confess or repent of them.

This is not true to the Holy Scriptures. Although the blood of Jesus does cleanse us of our present and future sin, it does not do so without confession and repentance (1 John 1:9; Rev. 2:5, 16, 21-22; Rev. 3:3, 19). We never have to be stuck with any sin, because the blood of Jesus continues to cleanse those who confess and repent.

In 1 John 1:9, the Bible makes it clear that "<u>If</u> (on the condition that) we confess our sins, He is faithful and just and will forgive us our sins and purify us from all unrighteousness."

Of course we all have sins we cannot confess, because we are not aware of them. Or perhaps we have forgotten them. I believe that if we are faithful to confess and repent of the sins we are aware of, that God honors the sincere and repentant heart and will cleanse us of the forgotten sins too. God always looks at the heart.

14. The good news is that all Christians can have the assurance of salvation.

God wants all who are in Christ Jesus to know for sure that they are saved and on their way to heaven:

1 John 5:11-13
11 And this is the testimony: **God has given us eternal life, and this life <u>is in his Son</u>**.
12 **He who has the Son has life**; he who does not have the Son of God does not have life.
13 I write these things to you who believe in the name of the Son of God **so that you may know that you have eternal life**.

Being that the assurance of eternal life is only for those who are <u>in</u> Jesus (verse 11), those who fail to remain in Him can have no assurance. This assurance is only for those who are "in the Son."

No one should ever presume that our holy God would allow those who abandon Jesus for a life of willful sin into His holy heaven. They are the ones who trample the Son of God under foot, counting His blood as an unholy thing (Heb. 10:26-29) and they can only expect "judgment and raging fire" (Heb. 10:26-27).

The good news is that all who have received Jesus as their Lord and Savior can know they are eternally secure as they remain in Him, who is the way, the truth and the life!

PART II

DEEPER INTO
THE SCRIPTURES

CHAPTER 11

What Christians Are
Likened To

I think in pictures. What I mean is that, when people speak to me, I often see what they are saying in my mind's eye. Having somewhat of a sense of humor, this can get me in trouble, especially when my wife is telling me something serious and I am picturing something humorous. Smiling when your spouse is saying something that is serious to her is not exactly the best way to enrich your marriage.

Now Jesus is my kind of teacher. I find the mental pictures He draws with His parables to be clear and precise, especially when He is explaining certain types of Christians. Although some of His parables are meant to encourage, most are warnings for us from a loving and caring Lord.

Jesus knows that we can too easily forget about certain ever-present dangers that are in our life. And let's not forget about the devil who is always looking for an opportunity to trap and destroy us. I would much rather be warned and corrected by Jesus than trapped and destroyed by the devil.

Jesus gives us the following parables as warnings for us concerning certain spiritual dangers. And, as a bonus, these parables reveal much truth about the security of the believer. So let's spend some time on these parables and see what Jesus has to say to us.

Jesus likens Christians to:

<u>Wise and Foolish Virgins</u>

I am glad that God gives wisdom to whoever asks by faith "without faultfinding" (James 1:5). We need wisdom! Especially when it comes to our walk and relationship with Jesus. The following parable is about wise and foolish virgins (Christians) who were betrothed to their bridegroom (Jesus). It is also a parable about the results of their different relationships with Jesus.

In the Parable of the Ten Virgins, Jesus is explaining what it will be like when He returns. Let's see what He says:

> Matt 25:1-13
> 1 At that time the **kingdom of heaven will be like ten virgins who took their lamps and went out to meet the bridegroom**.

Notice that all "ten virgins" were waiting for the bridegroom and all went out to meet Him, which tells us that all ten virgins are Christians of some sort. Unbelievers are not waiting for Jesus. In the Jewish culture, the bride would be the only "virgin" waiting for the bridegroom to take her to himself.

> 2 **Five of them were foolish and five were wise**…
> 3 **The foolish ones took their lamps but did not take any oil with them**.

98

What Christians are Likened To

In the Bible, oil represents the Holy Spirit. The foolish virgins in this parable had a little oil in their lamps (see verse eight), but not enough to keep their lamps going, for they took no extra oil with them. Evidently these virgins represent Christians who are distracted by the things of this world and have very little of the Holy Spirit in their life.

4 **The wise, however, took oil in jars along with their lamps.**

The wise virgins had plenty of oil. This tells us that they were filled with the Holy Spirit and maintained a strong relationship with their Lord. Jesus was first in their life.

5 The bridegroom was a long time in coming, and they all became drowsy and fell asleep.
6 At midnight the cry rang out: "Here's the bridegroom! Come out to meet him!"
7 Then all the virgins woke up and trimmed their lamps.
8 The foolish ones said to the wise, "Give us some of your oil; **our lamps are going out.**"

The foolish virgins' lamps were "going out," which meant they would not be ready for Jesus' return. It sounds to me like so many Christians who are trying to get by with a very weak commitment to Jesus; therefore their relationship with Him is fizzling like a lamp with little oil.

9 "No," they replied, "there may not be enough for both us and you. Instead, **go to those who sell oil and buy some for yourselves.**"

Spiritual zeal cannot be borrowed or bought…it is the result of a close, ongoing, trusting and obedient relationship with Jesus. At this point, there is no way for these lukewarm believers to immediately acquire the spiritual zeal that God requires at Jesus' return. I believe this is Jesus' way of warning that a person can wait too long to get his or her relationship right with Him.

> 10 But while they were on their way to buy the oil, the bridegroom arrived. **The virgins who were ready went in with him to the wedding banquet. And the door was shut.**

"And the door was shut" has such a sound of finality. Those who are ready will go in to be with Jesus. And what of those who are not ready for Jesus' return?

> 11 **Later the others** [foolish virgins] **also came. "Sir! Sir!"** [most versions say "Lord, Lord"] **they said. "Open the door for us!"**
> 12 **But he replied, "I tell you the truth, I don't know you."**

Ahhh, now we have the real problem with these locked-out, left-behind believers. Jesus did not know them because they had abandoned their relationship with Him. No doubt they were more interested in worldly pursuits than spending time with and following Jesus.

> 13 **Therefore keep watch, because you do not know the day or the hour.**

Who is this warning for? Remember, Jesus is talking to His disciples (or apostles) here. Would they be considered Christians? Of course they would…they had given up all to follow Jesus. Therefore, this parable is encouraging Christians to "keep oil in their lamps" and to maintain their relationship with Jesus so they will be ready for His return.

What Christians are Likened To

This parable puts new urgency to the Lord's command to "keep your spiritual zeal, serving the Lord" (Rom. 12:11) and His command to "be filled with the Holy Spirit" (Eph. 5:18). It is much better to wake up spiritually now than to be left out or behind later, which can be another tragic result of being lukewarm.

If you have been a foolish virgin, now is the time to wake up and get your relationship with Jesus right...before it's too late. If you are a wise virgin, you have nothing to worry about and much to look forward to.

Faithful or Lazy Servants

In this parable, Jesus tells us about two types of servants. Both types of servants belonged to the same Master and both types were entrusted with "talents" to use for their Master's interests. Let's take one or two verses at a time:

> Matt. 25:14-15, 19-30
> 14 Again, it [the kingdom of heaven] will be like a man going on a journey, who **called his servants** and **entrusted his property to them**.

Of course, the Master is Jesus and, therefore, His servants must be Christians, for they belonged to Him and He had entrusted His "talents" with them. Unbelievers are not considered servants of Jesus, nor does Jesus entrust spiritual gifts and abilities to unbelievers. The Master went on a journey and left His property in the hands of His servants, just as Jesus has gone into heaven and has entrusted the advancement of the gospel to us (Jude 3).

> 15 To one he gave **five talents** of money, to another **two talents**, and to another **one talent**, each according to his ability. Then he went on his journey...

A "talent" is a sum of money, but these talents can also be likened to gifted abilities Jesus has given to those who belong to Him. Every Christian has gifts...some have more and others less.

> 19 After a long time **the master of those servants returned** and settled accounts with them...
> 20 The **man who had received the five talents** brought the other five. "Master," he said, "you entrusted me with five talents. See, I have gained five more."
> 21 His master replied, **"Well done, good and faithful servant!** You have been faithful with a few things; I will put you in charge of many things. **Come and share your master's happiness!"**

As Jesus promised, He will return. And the time will come when all Christians will have to give an account for what they have done with the gifts God has given them. In this parable, the man that was given "five talents" used the abundance that God had given him for His glory and therefore received great reward for his faithfulness. This will be the glorious outcome of those who love and serve Jesus while on this earth.

But what of the Christian who is less gifted...the two-talent Christian?

> 22 The man with the **two talents** also came. "Master," he said, "you entrusted me with two talents; see, **I have gained two more."**
> 23 His master replied, **"Well done, good and faithful servant!** You have been faithful with a few things; I will put you in charge of many things. **Come and share your master's happiness!"**

This man did not receive as many talents (or abilities) as the man with five talents, but he faithfully used the little he had for his Master's glory. Not all Christians have the same abilities and gifts and so Jesus does not expect the same out of each. But notice, in verse 23, that the man who received only two talents received the same reward as the man who had received five talents. Those who have less, but give and use what they have for Jesus' glory, will receive the same reward as those who have been given more. God rewards Christians not for the amount of ability they have, but for their faithfulness and love for Him.

But then there are those worldly servants who do not use even the little they have to serve Jesus:

> 24 Then the man who had received the **one talent** came. "Master," he said, "I knew that you are a hard man, harvesting where you have not sown and gathering where you have not scattered seed.
> 25 So I was afraid and went out and **hid your talent in the ground**. See, here is what belongs to you."

This fellow had some flaky excuses for failing to serve Jesus. There will be those who have received Jesus, but then go through life doing their own thing, giving no thought to serving Him with what they have. Perhaps they have a false sense of security, thinking, "Well, I have received Jesus, so I am saved no matter what I do or don't do. So why worry about serving the Lord?"

But what will Jesus say to those "worthless" (verse 30) servants who do not use even the little God has given them for His glory?

> 29 His master replied, **"You wicked, lazy <u>servant</u>...**
> 30 ...throw that worthless <u>servant</u> outside, into the darkness, where there will be weeping and gnashing of teeth."**

According to Jesus, Christians who fail to serve Him with even the little God has given them will not be welcomed into His eternal kingdom. Jesus calls this servant wicked and lazy, and then gives instructions to throw him outside, into the darkness, where there will be weeping and gnashing of teeth.

Some will protest this interpretation while claiming that the servant with one talent was never saved in the first place. However, those who do this will have to ignore the rest of God's Word in order to make those Jesus calls His servants and entrusts with His talents unbelievers. They are Christians who have turned "wicked and lazy."

Others will say, "Isn't that teaching salvation by works?" They will have to talk to Jesus about that…He is the One who gave the parable. And I am sure He is not advocating salvation by works. Serving Jesus is not a work, but a love-response to the One who died for us. Jesus is just making it clear that those who belong to Him are expected to live for Him. Jesus paid a heavy price, not only so we could be forgiven, but also that we would love and serve Him:

> 1 Cor. 6:19-20
> 19 Do you not know that your body is a temple of the Holy Spirit, who is in you, whom you have received from God? **You are not your own**;
> 20 **you were bought at a price. Therefore honor God with your body**.

Instead of the focus being on "once saved, always saved," it should be on "once saved, always serve." There can be no security for those who have received Jesus, and then do their own selfish, worldly thing.

Remember Peter's words:

> 2 Peter 1:10-11
> 10 Therefore, my brothers, be all the more eager to **make your calling and election sure**. For <u>**if you do these things**</u>**, you will never fall**,
> 11 **and you will receive a rich welcome into the eternal kingdom** of our Lord and Savior Jesus Christ.

104

What Christians are Likened To

If doing things to make our calling and election sure is salvation by works, then the Lord's Apostle taught salvation by works, and we know he did not. So what does this tell us? It tells us that not only are we saved by grace through faith aside from works, but we also are saved by grace through faith "to do good works, which God prepared in advance for us to do."

> Eph. 2:8-10
> 8 For it is by grace you have been saved, through faith —
> and this not from yourselves, it is the gift of God—
> 9 not by works, so that no one can boast.
> 10 For we are God's workmanship, **created in Christ Jesus to do good works, which God prepared in advance for us to do.**

It amazes me how often verse ten is left out when the above verses are quoted. Once we are saved we must bear fruit for God. Good works are simply the fruit of maintaining a personal relationship with our Lord. He is our Master and we are His servants, therefore obedience, which produces a fruit-filled life, is simply a love-response to the King of Kings.

The servant with one talent had a sinful, lackadaisical attitude about serving Jesus, and the result was eternal rejection as a "wicked and lazy servant" (Matt. 25:26 and 30). Any Christian who chooses to serve the world and self over Jesus is in danger of the same outcome.

Salt That Can Become Worthless - Is There Such a Thing as an "Ex-Christian?"

I love salt and I probably use more of it than I should. Jesus loves salt too. He loves the kind of salt we are supposed to be…salty salt. So Jesus says:

Matt. 5:13

"You are the salt of the earth. But **if the salt loses its saltiness**, how can it be made salty again? **It is no longer good for anything**, except to be thrown out and trampled by men."

Salt is used for many purposes. It adds flavor to and preserves food and it may even have been used for antiseptic purposes in Jesus' time. But there is something in this verse that often puzzled me…that is until I did some research on salt.

What puzzled me was, "How in the world can salt lose its saltiness?" Being that Jesus used this terminology to describe something that can happen to Christians, I knew it must be possible.

After doing some research, I found that there is only one way for salt to lose its saltiness. Its physical composition would have to be changed through some chemical process. So, salt can lose its saltiness, but the result of such a chemical process would change salt into something other than what it once was. What was once salt would then become "ex-salt."

Of course, Jesus being God in the flesh knew this. So, when Jesus talks about Christians losing their saltiness, He is talking about Christians who have experienced a serious inner core change…a change of heart and soul. They have allowed worldly ideas, a lukewarm attitude and/or the constant indulgence of sinful desires to change their innermost being and have become something other than what they were created in Christ Jesus to be. As a result of this inner change, they have ceased to be Christians and have become "ex-Christians." Therefore, in the same way that salt can lose its saltiness and become "ex-salt," Christians can lose their heart for Jesus and become "ex-Christians."

Such "Christians" no longer have God's intended effect on this world, just as salt that has lost its saltiness does not have God's intended effect on whatever it touches. These salt-less people, who still call themselves Christians, bring shame to the name of Jesus by the way they live. According to this parable, they "are no longer good for anything" but "to be trampled by men."

Isn't it sad that so many people have had bad experiences with hypocritical Christians? And, as a result, they think all Christians are hypocrites and express total disdain for them. Then they verbally trample such "Christians" under foot, and worse yet, they conclude that Jesus is a farce. I know by experience that they are the most difficult people to witness to.

I know it is hard for those who believe once saved, always saved to accept that there is such a thing as an "ex-Christian," however, we must accept what God's Word says about Christians losing their saltiness. Ex-Christians who claim to be Christians cause more harm than we can imagine.

Fruitful or Unfruitful Branches

All of chapter five was dedicated to Jesus' teaching on the True Vine, so we will not go into John 15:1-6 in depth here. However, I must touch on these verses, because this passage does liken Christians to two types of branches.

> John 15:2 and 5-6
> 2 **He** [the Father] **cuts off every branch in me that bears no fruit,** while **every branch that does bear fruit he prunes so that it will be even more fruitful.**
> 5 I [Jesus] am the vine; you [Christians] are the branches. **If a man remains in me** and I in him, **he will bear much fruit**; apart from me you can do nothing.
> 6 **If anyone does not remain in me, he is like a branch that is thrown away and withers; such branches are picked up, thrown into the fire and burned.**

It is obvious that Jesus is the True Vine and that both the fruitful and fruitless branches are <u>in</u> Him. Therefore both are Christians. As I have already pointed out, no one can be in Jesus without being a born-again Christian. I emphasize this because there are those who believe that these fruitless "branches," who are <u>in Jesus</u>, were never truly saved in the first place. That is not possible.

Jesus' teaching on the True Vine creates a problem for those who cling to the once saved, always saved doctrine. If they acknowledge that these fruitless branches are in Jesus, as Jesus says they are, they will also be acknowledging that it is possible for a Christian to be "cut off" from Him, "thrown into the fire and burned," which is what Jesus says in verse six. And if they do that, they will in turn be acknowledging that a person who was once saved can again be lost.

Contradicting Jesus is a serious offense, as is falling away from the Lord. Falling away always yields disastrous results. And so, in the next chapter, we will be digging into the many passages where God warns us about "falling away" and "wandering" from the faith.

CHAPTER 12

Falling Away and Wandering From the Faith

I have had many encounters with Christians who believe once saved, always saved. Some truly love Jesus and hate sin, and others say they love Jesus but use this doctrine as a license to sin. All seem to think that falling away or wandering from the faith is not detrimental to the salvation of those who had truly received Jesus at some time in their life.

Many believe that backslidden Christians will eventually return to Jesus if they are really saved, thus their salvation is not in jeopardy. Some also believe, and teach, that if wayward Christians do not return to the Lord before they are taken from this earth they were never really saved in the first place. However, as I have pointed out before, this teaching cannot be found anywhere in the Bible and, therefore, it is unbiblical.

I am aware that not all who believe once saved, always saved believe exactly the same, but this is the most common feedback I get. However, I believe the most important question to be, "What does the Bible say about falling away and wandering from the faith?"

This chapter delves into many passages that warn Christians about falling from the faith at the expense of their salvation. Why would God give so many warnings if it were not possible for a Christian to forfeit his or her salvation? The sheer number of these passages should tell us how serious this subject is to God.

The Gospel Truth

<u>Warnings for Christians About Falling Away</u>

In Matthew 24, Jesus is talking to His disciples about the end times…what it will be like shortly before He returns.

Jesus' disciples, like many Christians today, were very interested in what will take place in the future. Just think how blessed they were to receive such vivid teaching on the end times right from the mouth of Jesus. But also think about how blessed we are. Here we are, over two thousand years later, watching much of what Jesus prophesied being fulfilled right before our very eyes.

About the end times, Jesus said:

> Matt. 24:10-13
> 10 At that time **many will turn away from the faith** and will betray and hate each other,
> 11 and many false prophets will appear and deceive many people.
> 12 Because of the **increase of wickedness, the love of most will grow cold,**
> 13 **but he who stands firm to the end will be saved.**

It is important to see that Jesus was not just talking about the condition of the world, but about the condition of the church in the last days. He told His disciples that "at that time many will fall away from the faith" and "the love of most will grow cold."

The picture Jesus draws of the church in the last days is not a pretty one, but it is a picture of what is taking place today. Jesus, being God manifested in the flesh, knows the future. The things He said would happen are happening.

We are experiencing a definite "increase of wickedness" and many Christians are being drawn into it. As a result, they are opting to live worldly, sinful, self-centered lives rather than the holy life God has called us to (Heb. 12:14). As a whole, the church has grown weak, because their love for the world has superseded their love for Jesus and the pursuit of holiness. Many who go to church on Sunday do not live for Jesus the rest of the week.

All we have to do is look at the high divorce rate in the church. It takes two to make a marriage work (not counting Jesus), but only one who is living for self to destroy it, leaving their spouse and children in emotional pain. Pain and sorrow is always the result of ignoring God's will and living for self.

Many who call themselves Christians are indulging in pornography, which often leads to physically cheating on their spouses. They cheat, they lie and they indulge their sinful desires, all while going to church. Will those who live like this be saved?

Jesus said that only "he who stands firm <u>to the end</u> will be saved," not those who come to the Lord, but later turn from Him to live in sin.

Luke 8:13
Those on the rock are **the ones who receive the word with joy** when they hear it, but they have no root. **They believe for a while**, but in the time of testing **they fall away**.

This verse is part of Jesus' explanation of the Parable of the Sower. In this verse, Jesus tells us that there are those who actually receive the word and believe for a while, but fall away in times of testing.

Some will say that those who fell away were never really saved in the first place. However, most Christians would agree that anyone who has <u>received the word</u> and <u>believed</u> for any amount of time would have to have been saved. Besides, Jesus also said they fell away…you cannot fall away from something you were never in. They were once saved and are now lost… and they will remain so unless they repent and return to Jesus.

111

Gal. 5:4-7

4 **You** who are trying to be justified by law **have been alienated from Christ; you have fallen away from grace**.

5 But by faith we eagerly await through the Spirit the righteousness for which we hope.

6 For in Christ Jesus neither circumcision nor uncircumcision has any value. The only thing that counts is faith expressing itself through love.

7 **You were running a good race. Who cut in on you and kept you from obeying the truth**?

Paul is speaking to Galatian Christians who had fallen from grace by embracing legalistic righteousness. They had actually chosen the law over Jesus and were even thinking of being circumcised. Doing so would seal their decision to live by the law rather than by faith in Jesus.

So Paul tells them:

Gal 5:2

Mark my words! I, Paul, tell you that if you let yourselves be circumcised, **Christ will be of no value to you at all**.

Wow! This is a serious warning. If Christ is of no value to someone, how can that person be saved?

Paul also warned that they had been "alienated from Christ." The word "alienated" means to be "separated from." In other words, they were once in Jesus, yet had separated themselves from Him. How can a person who has been separated from Jesus be saved, and how can a person be saved without the grace of God?

Falling Away and Wandering from the Faith

These Galatian Christians were walking on thin spiritual ice and, if they did not get back onto the solid Rock, they were sure to take a plunge in the sea of eternal destruction!

No one can expect salvation as a result of living by the law, observing legalistic righteousness or while willfully living in sin. All these things can separate us from Jesus and rob us of our inheritance in the kingdom of God. We must trust only in Jesus and follow Him as our sovereign Lord and Savior!

Gal. 5:19-21
19 The acts of the sinful nature are obvious: sexual immorality, impurity and debauchery;
20 idolatry and witchcraft; hatred, discord, jealousy, fits of rage, selfish ambition, dissensions, factions
21 and envy; drunkenness, orgies, and the like. **I warn you** [Galatian Christians], **as I did before**, that **those who live like this will not inherit the kingdom of God**.

God hates sin. He is a holy God who knows how destructive it is. His hatred of sin is seen throughout the Old Testament, and He has not weakened His stand since the time Jesus allowed Himself to be crucified to wash ours away.

In the above passage, Paul gives a long list of sinful activities that, if continued in, can disqualify Christians from partaking in the kingdom of God. Notice that Paul then says to these Galatian Christians, "I warn you...that those who live like this will not inherit the kingdom of God." Ignoring this warning can be eternally disastrous.

----

1 Tim. 1:18-20

113

18 Timothy, my son, I give you this instruction in keeping with the prophecies once made about you, so that by following them you may **fight the good fight**,
19 **holding on to faith** and a good conscience. **Some have rejected these** and so **have shipwrecked their faith.**
20 **Among them are Hymenaeus and Alexander,** whom **I have handed over to Satan** to be taught not to blaspheme.

2 Tim. 2:17-18
17 Their teaching will spread like gangrene. Among them are **Hymenaeus** and **Philetus,**
18 who have **wandered away from the truth.** They say that the resurrection has already taken place, and they destroy the faith of some.

2 Tim. 4:14
Alexander the metalworker did me a great deal of harm. **The Lord will repay him for what he has done.**

The above verses tell of three believers who caused Paul a great deal of trouble. Two of them, Hymenaeus and Alexander, are mentioned twice. Paul tells us that they had "shipwrecked their faith," which led him to hand them over to Satan (1 Tim. 1:19-20).

The word "shipwrecked" means to "ruin utterly" or "an irretrievable loss." These believers had fallen so far that they were even blaspheming the Lord (1 Tim. 1:20), bringing their faith to utter ruin. I would not want to be in their spiritual shoes for anything.

It is sad, but these apostates were fulfilling the scriptures: "Of them the proverbs are true: 'A dog returns to its vomit,' and 'A sow that is washed goes back to her wallowing in the mud'" (2 Peter 2:22).

Falling Away and Wandering from the Faith

1 Tim. 4:1
The **Spirit clearly says** that in later times **some will abandon the faith** and follow deceiving spirits and things taught by demons.

Okay, God is telling us something that no one should have any trouble understanding. The Holy Spirit makes it clear that some will abandon the faith and follow deceiving spirits and things taught by demons. Obviously, a person cannot follow Jesus and deceiving spirits at the same time.

If I told you that someone has abandoned ship, you would readily understand that the person was once on the ship, but is no longer. It is the same with those who "abandon the faith." They were once in the faith, but are no longer.

So, being that the "Spirit clearly says" that a person can abandon the faith, it is equally clear that a person who was in the faith can again end up outside the faith. I am truly concerned for those who feel compelled to twist what the Holy Spirit clearly says to protect his or her stand on the security of the believer. It is a dangerous thing to contradict the Holy Spirit.

---

1 Tim. 6:8-12
8 But if we have food and clothing, we will be content with that.
9 **People who want to get rich fall into temptation and a trap** and into many foolish and harmful desires that plunge men into ruin and destruction.
10 For the love of money is a root of all kinds of evil. **Some people, eager for money, have wandered from the faith and pierced themselves with many griefs**.

115

11 **But you, man of God, flee from all this**, and pursue righteousness, godliness, faith, love, endurance and gentleness.
12 Fight the good fight of the faith. **Take hold of the eternal life to which you were called** when you made your good confession in the presence of many witnesses.

Here Paul warns Christians to avoid the love of money and encourages them to be content with what they have. He then points out that some who were eager for money had wandered from the faith and, thus, had created all kinds of griefs for themselves.

It is interesting that Paul talks about the danger of wandering from the faith in the same passage that he instructs Timothy to "take hold of the eternal life" to which he was called. Timothy already had eternal life, so why would Paul tell him to take hold of eternal life that he already had? There can be only two reasons for this:

1. Timothy was backsliding and Paul did not want to see his faith and eternal life slip away. I don't think this was the case, as the Scriptures never indicate that Timothy was a backslidden believer. So, more likely:

2. Paul wanted Timothy to keep a good grip on his eternal life by pursuing the right things (verse 11), because it is possible for it to slip away by pursuing the wrong things (verses 9-10).

If carnal Christians wander from the faith to pursue money at the expense of their relationship with Jesus, they are also letting go of the eternal life to which they have been called. Remember, Jesus said that it is those who "stand firm till the end" who will be saved. What could be clearer?

Those who abandon the faith to live for money, the world, self or sin are living on dangerous ground.

Falling Away and Wandering from the Faith

----

1 Tim. 6:20-21
20 Timothy, guard what has been entrusted to your care.
Turn away from godless chatter and the opposing ideas of
what is falsely called knowledge,
21 which some have professed and in so doing **have
wandered from the faith**. Grace be with you.

God also warns us that it is possible to wander from the
faith because of false doctrine. Watch out for any doctrine that
does not match up with God's Holy Word!

Heb. 3:12-14
12 See to it, **brothers**, that none of **you** has **a sinful,
unbelieving heart that turns away** from the living God.
13 But encourage one another daily, as long as it is called
Today, so that none of you may be hardened by **sin's
deceitfulness**.
14 **We have come to share in Christ if we hold firmly
till the end** the confidence we had at first.

The writer of Hebrews warns his Christian "brothers" not
to develop a sinful, unbelieving heart that turns away from the
living God. How deceitful sin is! How careful we must be not to
accept sin as the norm, least we develop "a sinful, unbelieving
heart that turns away from the living God." He also says, "we
have come to share in Christ **if** we hold firmly **till the end** the
confidence we had at first."

God again makes it clear that the condition to sharing in
Christ is that "we hold firmly till the end…" We must come to
Jesus by obedient faith, and we must remain in Jesus till the end
by that same faith. Christians who allow even the slightest sin to
abide in their hearts can pay a heavy price for their carelessness.

117

When I was very young, I once caught a lizard. Being a curious little guy, I decided to see what that lizard would do if I put it in a pot of cool water over a hot burner. Of course, my mother wasn't home at the time, and I assure you that giving this example does not mean I condone lizard boiling…I was just a kid!

Well, would you believe that lizard didn't even try to climb out of the pot…it just sat there and allowed itself to be boiled degree by degree. It didn't notice how hot it was getting until it was too late. That's the way it is with sin.

If you should ever sense that you are accepting any kind of sin in your life, no matter how trivial it may seem, repent and renew your relationship with Jesus immediately. Depend on the Holy Spirit for the power to overcome your sin and He will enable you. In time, you will have the victory. Remember that, "the one who is in you is greater than the one who is in the world" (1 John 4:4).

Rev. 3:5
He who overcomes will, like them, be dressed in white. **I will never blot out his name from the book of life**, but will acknowledge his name before my Father and his angels.

For some reason most people seem to think the Book of Revelation cannot be understood at all, as though it were the "Book of Concealment." Did God really go through all that trouble to give this revelation to John in order to puzzle and confuse His people? Some of this great book may be difficult to understand, but most of it, especially Jesus' instructions to the churches, contains very clear messages for the church today.

The first verse in this book tells us that it contains "The **revelation** of Jesus Christ, which God gave him **to show his**

servants what must soon take place..." This book was designed to reveal important truths to us.

The great message in this book came by way of personal revelation from Jesus to John the Apostle. Jesus told John to write on a scroll what he heard and saw. He was then told to send what he had written to the seven churches listed in Revelation 1:11. These messages were concerning their relationship with Him.

In these messages, Jesus rebuked five out of the seven churches. One of these churches was Sardis. As a part of His warning to this spiritually weak church, He told them that those who overcome would never have their name blotted out of the book of life (Rev. 3:5). Well, what about those who do not overcome? If those who overcome will not have their names blotted out of book of life, it stands to reason that those who do not overcome will have their names blotted out of the book of life.

However, there are Christians who insist that, because Jesus did not clearly state He would blot anyone's name from the book of life, He never will. Those who do this are ignoring the obvious at the expense of truth. The obvious is presented in these examples of proper reasoning:

If I were to say:	The logical conclusion would be:
"He who stays in the ship will not drown."	Those who do not stay in the ship might drown.
"The person who stays in the house during a storm will not get rained on."	The person who goes out of the house during a storm will get rained on.
"The person who has no baby will get more sleep."	The person who has a baby will get less sleep.
Therefore the same rule of logic should be applied to:	

"He who overcomes will not have his name blotted from the book of life."	Therefore, he who does not overcome will have his name blotted from the book of life.

All the above examples, including the last one, are just plain common sense. Jesus gave us Revelation 3:5 as both a warning and an encouragement.

Another "blotting" passage to consider is found in the book of Exodus:

> Ex. 32:32-33 [Moses speaking]
> 32 "But now, **please forgive their sin — but if not, then blot me out of the book you have written."**
> 33 The LORD replied to Moses, **"Whoever has sinned against me I will blot out of my book."**

Very clear, wouldn't you say? I think every Christian would agree that it is a shameful and dangerous thing to distort the obvious meaning of the text while putting other souls at risk.

Listen to this warning:

> Rev. 22:19
> And **if** anyone takes words away from this book of prophecy, **God will take away from him his share in the tree of life and in the holy city**, which are described in this book.

You must have eternal life to have a "share in the tree of life and in the holy city" that is to come. However, the above verse tells us that a person who has a "share in the tree of life" (eternal life) can lose his share by distorting God's Word, particularly the words in the Book of Revelation. If a person's share in the tree of life and their place in the holy city are taken away, there is no place for them in the presence of God.

Falling Away and Wandering from the Faith

The only honest conclusion we can arrive at from the above verses is that God will blot Christians who choose to live in sin out of His book. The best way to guard against falling into such a state of apostasy is to stay close to Jesus and to hate sin with a passion no matter what you believe about the security of the believer. God has given us the Holy Spirit so that we can be victorious…and if you walk in the Spirit, you will be!

Many Christians may have difficulty accepting that the warnings found in this chapter are actually for born-again Christians. While some will accept them, others will ignore them. Some will even distort them to fit their belief.

I have personally seen otherwise good Bible teachers do this many times. However, there are many other verses and passages in the Bible that must be "adjusted" in order to preserve the once saved, always saved doctrine. And so, in the next chapter, we will study some of the most often ignored and distorted passages in the Bible…passages that clearly contradict the once saved, always saved doctrine.

CHAPTER 13

Undeniable but Often Abused Passages

Before going into full-time ministry, I was a carpenter and general contractor for a total of eighteen years. During that time, there was one thing I was strongly aware of…the importance of laying a straight, level foundation.

You see, if you build a house on a "roller-coaster," crooked foundation, the rest of the house will never be right. The distorted foundation will cause problems with everything from setting the cabinets to ending up with rain gutters that overflow on one end when storms hit. Once the foundation is off, the best you can do is to adjust the framework so that the house will look right on the outside…but it will never be right.

That's how it is with the once saved, always saved doctrine. The clear meaning of certain scriptures must continually be "adjusted" in order to make it "look right." During my 41 years of being a Christian, I have often been puzzled by otherwise solid, Jesus-loving teachers adjusting the obvious meaning of the Scriptures to preserve this doctrine.

I don't believe those who do this do it for unethical reasons. However, starting with a strongly-held, preconceived belief will always affect the way Bible students approach God's Word. And, of course, that will in turn also affect their conclusions. Preserving the clear meaning of God's Word is eternally more important than preserving what we have always believed. What the Bible says should always determine our beliefs and not the other way around.

So, in this chapter we will examine, in expository style, many undeniable, but often-abused passages that deal with salvation, eternal life and the security of the believer. Please examine these passages with an open heart and mind.

The Gospel of John

John 15:1-6

Yes, I know…I already covered this portion of Scripture thoroughly in chapter five. However, I must at least make reference to John 15:1-6 as being one of the most abused passages in the Bible. The clear meaning of this passage is often manipulated or ignored because of its clarity concerning the security of the believer.

In John 15, Jesus makes it clear that a believer is only secure as he or she "remains" in Him, and that it is every bit possible for an unfruitful Christian to be "cut off [from Jesus]…thrown into the fire and burned" (verse six). The bottom line is that salvation is found only in Jesus. Therefore, there can be no salvation for those who were once in Him, but have since abandoned Him for a disobedient, unfruitful life. So, if you haven't already done so, be sure to go back and read chapter five. You will get the truth straight from the heart and mouth of Jesus.

If you have already read chapter five, let's move on and see what Paul wrote to the Christians in Rome concerning the security of the believer.

The Book of Romans

We will start off with the eleventh chapter of the book of Romans where Paul is addressing the Gentile believers. A Gentile is anyone who is not a Jew. Here Paul reminds these believers that, although Israel is presently lost and cut off from God's grace and salvation, God still loves Israel and has a plan for their restoration. Paul also tells us that there is still a remnant of Jews who have turned to Jesus and are saved (Rom. 11:5).

However, the focus of a portion of this chapter is on the salvation that comes from being connected to God's "root." Hmmm, who or what must we be connected to in order to have salvation? Is it Israel or is it Jesus? Not only is Jesus our only source of salvation, but He is also the only one that enables us to bear fruit for God's glory by providing the Holy Spirit.

Who can deny that the Holy Spirit comes from both the Father and the Son? And who can deny that Jesus imparts and baptizes with the Holy Spirit (John 20:22; Matt. 3:11)? And who can deny that the Holy Spirit empowers us to live and bear fruit for God's glory just as the sap of a tree empowers its branches to bear fruit? Those who are in Jesus have a source of spiritual strength and power that would make the atomic bomb look like a firecracker. That is why the Bible tells us that we can do all things through Him who gives us the strength (Phil. 4:13). Just cling to Jesus and let Him fill you with the Holy Spirit.

<u>Romans 11:16-26</u>

This passage has been interpreted, and misinterpreted, in many ways. One reason for this is that this passage was written to a now-ancient culture, and parts of it can be difficult for modern-day Christians to understand, especially when taken out of context. Another reason this passage is so often misinterpreted is that it contains verses that, if taken at face value, solidly refute the once saved, always saved doctrine.

So, in order to avoid any distortion on our part, let's consider those things that are easy to understand, and let's take them at face value.

We will take one or two verses at a time:

16 If the part of the dough offered as firstfruits is holy, then the whole batch is holy; if the root is holy, so are the branches.

Paul reminds these Roman believers of a very simple spiritual principle. He tells them that if part of the dough taken from the batch is holy, then the whole batch must be holy. That would be like saying that if a sip from a glass of lemonade is sweet then the whole glass of lemonade must be sweet. Common sense.

Then, using the same reasoning, he explains that "if the root is holy" then the branches that are connected to the root, via the tree, must also be holy. The conclusion we can easily come to from this verse is that holy things come from holy sources. I believe this to be the message God wants to give us from this verse.

Although the principle is clear, you will notice that Paul never tells us exactly what the root or the branches are. We will have to arrive at these conclusions based on what he says in the following verses.

17 If some of the branches have been broken off, and **you, though a wild olive shoot, have been grafted in** among the others and now share in the **nourishing sap from the olive root**,

Before we go on, I want to point out that there are two opposing views about who or what the root in verse 16 is, and one thing most Christians agree on:

1. Some Christians believe the "root" in verse 16 represents Israel.
2. Other Christians believe the "root" in verse 16 represents Jesus.
3. Most agree that the "wild olive shoot" (a new branch) refers to Gentile Christians.

Undeniable but Often Abused Passages

Knowing these wild olive shoots are Christians makes determining who or what the root is a lot easier. All we have to do is ask, "In whom or what are Christians rooted into that makes them holy before God?" Believing that this root is Israel leads to some erroneous conclusions that we cannot escape:

a. If we Gentile Christians have been grafted into Israel, then we are just as dependent on Israel for life as a branch is dependent on its root.

b. If we Gentile Christians have been grafted into Israel, we are also dependent on Israel's "nourishing sap" for spiritual life, and for everything else we need to bear fruit for God.

Now, I don't know about you, but I do not depend on Israel for any of these things. Nor do I consider Israel my source of spiritual life. Jesus is my source and my life. I receive all I need for life and godliness from Him and Him alone. I cannot possibly see how the "root" in this verse can be anything but Jesus, who is God's covenant provision for all who trust in Him.

However, the Jews, God's original covenant people, clung to the law and rejected Jesus, and were therefore cut off from God's New Covenant provision. That's why Paul tells us that "some branches were broken off" and we were "grafted in."

Thinking that the Jews were "broken off" from God's source of spiritual life so that the Gentiles could be grafted in (see verses 19-20 below) must have given some of these Gentile believers a big head. So Paul says:

18 **do not boast over those branches**. If you do, consider this: You do not support the root, but the root supports you.

Dear Christian, who supports you? Is it Israel? Certainly not! It is Jesus, who is our very life!

19 You will say then, "Branches were broken off so that I could be grafted in."
20 Granted. But **they were broken off because of unbelief, and you stand by faith.** Do not be arrogant, but **be afraid.**

What were the Jews "broken off" of by their unbelief? Was it not God's plan of salvation that was to come through believing in, receiving and abiding in Jesus? They rejected the Messiah they were waiting for. And in whom do we stand by faith? Not Israel. We stand by faith in Jesus alone!

However, the Jews could not bring themselves to trust in Jesus. They stumbled over the "Stumbling Stone" (faith in Jesus as the Messiah):

Rom 9:30-33
30 What then shall we say? That the Gentiles, who did not pursue righteousness, have obtained it, a righteousness that is by faith;
31 but Israel, who pursued a law of righteousness, has not attained it.
32 Why not? Because they pursued it not by faith but as if it were by works. **They stumbled over the "stumbling stone."**
33 As it is written: "See, I lay in Zion a stone that causes men to stumble and a rock that makes them fall, and **the one who trusts in him will never be put to shame."**

There is only one way for both Jews and Gentiles to be grafted into Jesus, who is not only the Root of Jesse and David (Rev. 5:5; 15:12) but also God's True Vine. All must come to Him by faith alone (Eph. 2:8). By faith we receive Jesus as our Lord and Savior, and by faith we live and stand in Him.

But now we must ask why, in Romans 11:20, did Paul warn these Gentile believers not to "be arrogant," but to "be afraid"? Here is Paul's answer:

21 For **if God did not spare the natural branches, he will
not spare you either**.

If God did not spare the natural branches from what? From
being "broken off" from God's ultimate plan of salvation for
His people. And so God makes it clear that Christians who
abandon the faith can be broken off and end up just as lost as
the unbelieving Jews were! So Paul advises these believers to:

22 Consider therefore the kindness and sternness of God:
sternness to those who fell, but **kindness to you,
provided that you continue in his kindness.
Otherwise, you also will be cut off**.

The language in this passage is clear. "Continue in His
kindness, otherwise you also will be cut off" just as the Jews
were. Being cut off is something any sensible Christian should
be afraid of (see verse 20).

Developing a sinful, unbelieving heart after coming to Jesus
can sever Christians from Him. We should avoid anything that
draws us away from Jesus for fear of the disastrous results.
However, as long as we stay close to and remain in Jesus
through a trusting and obedient life, there is nothing to fear.

But what of Christians who abandon Jesus, but later regret
their sins and repent? Is there any hope to be grafted back into
Him as a result of earnest repentance? Let's see:

23 And **if they do not persist in unbelief, they will be
grafted in**, for God is able to graft them in again.

The Jews were broken off from God because of unbelief,
however, this verse goes on to tell us that the Jews can be
grafted back into their relationship with God through faith. Of
course, that faith must be in Jesus, who will bring them into a
New Covenant relationship with God. And so it is clear that

Jews who were once broken off from God by unbelief can be restored again (grafted back in) by repentance and turning to Jesus as their Lord and Savior. I believe God holds out the same hope for believers who have abandoned Jesus…that is unless they reach the place of no return mentioned in Hebrews 6:4-6, and only God knows when that is.

> 24 After all, if you were cut out of an olive tree that is wild by nature, and contrary to nature were grafted into a cultivated olive tree, how much more readily will these, the natural branches, be grafted into their own olive tree!
> 25 I do not want you to be ignorant of this mystery, brothers, so that you may not be conceited: **Israel has experienced a hardening in part until the full number of the Gentiles has come in.**

The time will come when the full number of the Gentiles will be reached for salvation. Only God knows what that number is, but it can happen at any time. Once the full number of Gentiles is reached, God will turn His attention back to the salvation of Israel:

> 26 And so all Israel **will be saved**, as it is written: "The deliverer will come from Zion; he will turn godlessness away from Jacob."

The Book of Hebrews

The book of Hebrews was written to Christians by a Christian. The way the writer addresses these people makes this clear:

> Heb. 3:1
> Therefore, **holy brothers**, who **share in the heavenly calling**, fix your thoughts on **Jesus, the apostle and high priest whom <u>we</u> confess**.

Only true believers could possibly be considered holy brothers who share in the heavenly calling while confessing Jesus as their high priest. And so the book of Hebrews was definitely written to and for believers.

This is important to see, because some who believe once saved, always saved claim that certain passages in Hebrews were written to non-Christians. Perhaps the reason for this is that these passages, when properly applied to believers, contradict the once saved, always saved doctrine.

Let's take a look at some of these passages:

<u>Hebrews 6:4-12</u>

I can give you five characteristics of just about any creature on God's earth and you would be able to tell me what it is. If I were to tell you "It walks on four legs, sometimes bites, wags its tail, loves its master and barks," you would have no problem identifying what it is. Or if I told you "It is very large, it's gray, very strong, has tusks and a trunk," you would have no problem identifying that one either. Well, the following verses give us five characteristics of those who "are crucifying the Son of God all over again" (verse six), making it clear who they are:

> 4 It is impossible for those who **have once been enlightened**, who **have tasted the heavenly gift**, who have **shared in the Holy Spirit**,
> 5 who have **tasted the goodness of the word of God** and **the powers of the coming age**,
> 6 if **they fall away**, to be brought back to repentance, because to their loss **they are crucifying the Son of God** all over again and **subjecting him to public disgrace**.

So these people:

1. Have once been enlightened.

2. Have shared in the Holy Spirit.
3. Have tasted God's heavenly gift.
4. Have tasted the goodness of the Word of God.
5. Have tasted the powers of the coming age.

Now, if I were to tell any objective Christian that Joe Shmoe has been enlightened by God's Word, has shared in the Holy Spirit, has tasted (Greek: "experienced") God's heavenly gift, has tasted (experienced) the goodness of God's Word and the powers of the coming age, he or she could readily identify this person as a born-again Christian.

However, in spite of the distinctly Christian characteristics enumerated in Hebrews 6:4-6, many Christians have great difficulty accepting that these verses could possibly be describing those who had once been Christians. If they did, due to the context, they would in turn be acknowledging that saved people could again be lost forever due to their own foolish choices.

Being that this passage is so difficult for some Christians to understand or accept, let's dig in a little deeper, taking one portion at a time.

These people:

"have once been enlightened." (verse four)

Only Christians have "been enlightened" by the Holy Spirit. Before coming to Jesus, we were spiritually blind and unable to see the truth. But Jesus sent the Holy Spirit to open our eyes...I once was blind, but now I see.

"have shared in the Holy Spirit." (verse four)

When a person is saved, Jesus gives him or her the Holy Spirit. Therefore, all believers share in the Holy Spirit and are to live by Him (Gal. 4:6; 1 Cor. 3:16). Unbelievers have no share in the Holy Spirit…He is only for true believers.

"have __tasted__ the heavenly gift." (verse four)

NT:1089 geuomai (ghyoo'-om-ahee); a primary verb; to taste; by implication, to eat; figuratively, to experience (good or ill) (Strong's Greek/Hebrew)

Only Christians "have tasted the heavenly gift" of God. Being that the word "tasted" figuratively means experienced in the Greek, some versions use the word "experienced" in place of tasted.

To my astonishment, I have heard some say that these people were not true believers because "they only 'tasted' the heavenly gift, but did not swallow it." Those who do this apparently ignore the true meaning of the word "tasted" and the obvious meaning of the text and context because it does not fit what they already believe.

Since when does God give people just a taste of salvation so they can try the heavenly gift out before they swallow it? You either receive Jesus by faith or you don't. Personally, I think God's heavenly gift tastes a lot better than the life I lived before coming to Jesus!

"have tasted the goodness of the Word of God and the powers of the coming age." (verse five)

These people had also tasted the goodness of the Word of God and the powers of the coming age. No one can say for sure what is meant by tasting the powers of the coming age. However, we do know that if anyone has "tasted the goodness of the Word of God," they have experienced a personal relationship with Jesus, for He is the Word who was with God in the beginning (John 1:1-2, 14). Indeed, the Holy Spirit is warning Christians that "it is impossible" (verse four) that:

> 6 if **they fall away**, to be brought back to repentance, because to their loss **they are crucifying the Son of God** all over again and **subjecting him to public disgrace**.

Being that the word "if" at the beginning of this verse is not in the original Greek, Young's Literal Translation rightly translates it:

> 6 and **having fallen away**, again to renew [them] to reformation, **having crucified again to themselves the Son of God**, and **exposed to public shame**. YLT

According to Young's Literal Translation, "and having fallen away" is closer to the intended meaning of this verse than "if they fall away," which makes it clear that this falling away has already taken place.

If I were to tell you I fell off a bike that I was never on, you would think I was a little crazy. You cannot fall off something you were never on. In the same way, you cannot fall away from Jesus unless you have been in Him in the first place.

So, those spoken of in this verse were definitely fallen Christians who are "crucifying the Son of God all over again and subjecting Him to public disgrace (or shame)." Only fallen Christians can do this. They expose Jesus to public shame by misrepresenting Him to this world. Unbelievers cannot misrepresent Jesus, for they do not belong to Him.

Also notice, in verses 4-6, that Christians who have fallen away can come to a place where it is impossible for them to be brought back to repentance, which cannot be said about unbelievers. The door to repentance and salvation is always open to unbelievers.

Now the writer of Hebrews repeats what he just said in parable form:

7 **Land that drinks in the rain** often falling on it and that **produces a crop** useful to those for whom it is farmed **receives the blessing of God.**

Verses 4-6 make it clear that this passage is talking about Christians. In keeping with the context, the "land" in verse seven represents faithful Christians and the rain represents all that God gives them so they can bear fruit for His glory. Christians who bear good fruit because they remain in Jesus will receive a blessing from God. But what of Christians who desert Jesus for a life of sin?

8 But **land that produces thorns and thistles is worthless** and is **in danger of being cursed. In the end it will be burned.**

The land that produces thorns and thistles represents Christians who choose sin over Jesus. They are harmful to God's cause and, according to God's Word, they are "worthless" and in danger of being "cursed" and "burned." (This passage parallels John 15:5-6 perfectly.)

9 Even though we speak like this, dear friends, **we are confident of better things in your case** — things that accompany salvation.
10 God is not unjust; he will not forget your work and the love you have shown him as you have helped his people and continue to help them.

Although the writer of Hebrews was confident that those he was writing to would not end up as apostates, he warned them of the possibility.

11 We want each of you to show this same **diligence <u>to the very end, in order to make your hope sure</u>.**

135

It is interesting that the writer of Hebrews tells Christians they need to be diligent to the very end in order to make their hope sure. Obviously, those who abandon Jesus are not diligent to the end and cannot be sure of their hope of eternal life. In other words, Christians must stick in there with Jesus to the end to have this sure hope.

Jesus said the same thing when He prophesied: "many will fall away from the faith" and "the love of most will grow cold, but **he who stands firm to the end will be saved**" (Matthew 24:10-13).

It is not those who begin the race who get the prize, but those who finish the race. It is not those who begin the Christian voyage, but those who are still on board at the end of the journey that will reach their heavenly destination. Only those who remain in Jesus "to the very end" will be saved. And so the writer of Hebrews admonishes these believers by saying:

> 12 We do not want you to become lazy, but to imitate **those who through faith and patience inherit what has been promised**.

Hebrews 6:4-12 is a clear and powerful passage. Yet, there is another portion of Scripture in the Book of Hebrews that is equally or perhaps even more troublesome when it comes to the once saved, always saved doctrine:

Hebrews 10:26-31

Again, we will take one or two verses at a time to draw the purest meaning possible from this very revealing passage:

> 26 If <u>we</u> deliberately keep on sinning after we have received the knowledge of the truth, no sacrifice for sins is left,
> 27 but only a **fearful expectation of judgment and of raging fire** that will consume the **enemies of God**.

In this sober warning, the writer includes himself by saying, "If **we**." Therefore, it is undeniable that Hebrews 10:26-31 applies to those who are born-again Christians.

According to verses 26-27, Christians who deliberately keep on sinning after receiving the knowledge of truth are in danger of God's judgment and raging fire that will consume the enemies of God. It is important to see that these verses are not talking about the sin we occasionally stumble into and then repent of, but the willful choice to "deliberately keep on sinning" that puts Christians into a dangerous state of apostasy (verse 26).

Falling into sin and then repenting as soon as you are convicted by the Holy Spirit is a lot different than willfully choosing to continue in sin. Jesus will not tolerate deliberate, continual sin. Christians who choose to live in sin over living for Jesus choose eternal death over eternal life. One cannot live for Jesus and live in sin at the same time.

We find a similar warning from James when he says, "You adulterous people, don't you know that friendship with the world is hatred toward God? Anyone who chooses to be a friend of the world becomes an enemy of God" (James 4:4).

Adultery seems to be no big deal to a large percentage of our society. Many say it's wrong, but their lives say differently. However, adultery is a big deal to Jesus...especially when it's His bride committing it. Adultery is having an intimate relationship with someone outside of the one you are bound to. As Christians, we are bound to Jesus. Therefore, James warns us against loving and putting the sinful activities of this world before Jesus. He then makes it clear that the Christian who does can "become an enemy of God." And so, a child of God can become an enemy of God by putting the world and sin before Jesus.

Most who say a Christian cannot stop being a child of God liken the spiritual birth to the physical birth. However, the physical birth is one of flesh and blood, and the spiritual birth is based on a relationship with Jesus Christ, which can be abandoned by choosing this sinful world over Him.

Now, in Hebrews 10, God tells us why these Christians deserve to be "severely" punished:

> 28 Anyone who rejected the law of Moses died without mercy on the testimony of two or three witnesses.
> 29 How much **more severely do you think a man deserves to be punished** who has **trampled the Son of God under foot**, who has **treated as an unholy thing the blood of the covenant that sanctified him**, and who has **insulted the Spirit of grace**?

In the above verses we see three deadly sins that Christians who "deliberately keep on sinning" commit:

Deadly sin #1 - Trampling the Son of God under foot:

Verse 29 tells us that Christians who live for self and sin instead of Jesus "deserve to be punished" because they "trample the son of God under foot." In other words, Christians who deliberately keep on sinning after coming to Jesus are treating Him like dirt and will get what they deserve.

Deadly sin #2 - Treating the blood of Jesus that sanctified them as an unholy thing:

Verse 29 talks about people who had been "sanctified" by the blood of Jesus. The blood of Jesus sanctifies believers, not non-believers. So this verse is talking about believers who had deserted Jesus. As a result, they were treating the blood that had sanctified them as though it were "an unholy thing." How terrible! No wonder this verse tells us that they deserve to be punished "more severely."

Deadly sin #3 - Insulting the Spirit of Grace:

138

Undeniable but Often Abused Passages

Christians who choose sin over Jesus "deserve to be punished" because they "insult the Spirit of grace." God had poured out His Spirit of grace on them, and they snubbed the Holy Spirit as though He was nothing. What an insult to God! Therefore they will pay the price:

> 30 For we know him who said, "It is mine to avenge; I will repay," and again, "**The Lord will judge <u>his</u> people**."
> 31 It is a dreadful thing to fall into the hands of the living God.

So again we see that God will judge <u>His</u> people. These scriptures are not talking about judging unbelievers, but those who came to and then deserted Jesus.

2 Peter

Second Peter also contains passages that make it clear that Christians can abandon Jesus to their own eternal destruction. Let's dig in:

<u>2 Peter 1:10-11</u>

> 10 Therefore, my brothers, **be all the more eager to make your calling and election sure**. For **if** [on the condition that] **you do these things, you will never fall**,

Peter, the Lord's Apostle, teaches that there are certain things we should do to make our calling and election sure. (For a list of these things, see 2 Peter 1:5-9.) If I were to say what Peter said in most Christian circles, I would be accused of promoting salvation by works. But I am not the one who said this…it was the Lord's Apostle, speaking by the inspiration of the Holy Spirit.

If God instructs us to live in such a way to make our calling and election sure, then it is obviously possible to live in such a way to render our calling and election unsure.

Verse 10 also says, "…if you do these things, you will never fall." Therefore, it must be possible to fall if you fail to do these things. We are saved by grace, yet we can fall from grace by ignoring God's Word and the promptings of the Holy Spirit. That is the reason for Peter's sober warning.

Peter is not preaching a salvation by works. He is encouraging Christians to pursue godly characteristics that will give them spiritual stamina to "stand firm to the end" (Matt. 24:10-13). And here is the result of pursuing the godly characteristics mentioned in 2 Peter 1:5-9:

> 11 **and you will receive a rich welcome into the eternal kingdom** of our Lord and Savior Jesus Christ.

So, those who live for Jesus will receive a rich welcome into the eternal kingdom. But what of Christians who are not presently living for Jesus? What of those who make no effort to pursue the godly characteristics listed in 2 Peter 1:5-9, but, instead, pursue a life of sin without repentance? They will not receive a rich welcome into the eternal kingdom of our Lord and Savior, for they have "trampled the Son of God under foot" (Heb. 10:29).

2 Peter 2:20-22

I can't say that I like pigs, but I do like dogs. However, dogs can also have some pretty disgusting, even nauseating, habits. But, then again, so do Christians who have fallen away. Let's look at this whole passage and then break it down verse-by-verse:

> 20 If **they have escaped the corruption of the world by knowing our Lord and Savior Jesus Christ** and **are**

again entangled in it and overcome, **they are worse off at the end than they were at the beginning.**
21 **It would have been better for them not to have known the way of righteousness,** than to have known it and then to turn their backs on the sacred command that was passed on to them.
22 Of them the proverbs are true: **"A dog returns to its vomit,"** and, **"A sow that is washed goes back to her wallowing in the mud."**

Starting with verse 20, God describes Christians who return to the corruption of the world, and it's not a pretty picture:

20 **If they have escaped the corruption of the world** by **knowing our Lord and Savior Jesus Christ** and **are again entangled in it and overcome,** they are **worse off at the end than they were at the beginning.**

The people being described in the above verse had "escaped the corruption of the world by <u>knowing</u> our Lord and Savior Jesus Christ." If that does not describe a Christian, I do not know what does. Jesus said that to know Him is eternal life (John 17:3). Therefore, these born-again Christians had gone astray and are again "entangled" in the corruption of the world.

Then Peter says these amazing words: "they are worse off at the end than they were at the beginning." Wow! Who can be worse off than someone who has never come to Jesus? These Christians who had deserted Jesus to go back to a life of sin, were "worse off" after receiving Him than before coming to Him. And how can anyone who has been saved be worse off than before they were saved?

Remember that, in speaking of Christians who have turned from Jesus to sin, Hebrews 10:29 asks, "How much more severely do you think a man deserves to be punished who has trampled the Son of God under foot, who has treated as an unholy thing the blood of the covenant that sanctified him, and who has insulted the Spirit of grace?" God has determined that Christians who do such things deserve to be punished "<u>more severely</u>" than those who never received Jesus in the first place. Hell is a horrible place of punishment. Evidently God has something extra unpleasant planned for those who treat Jesus so shamefully. They will indeed be worse off at the end than they were at the beginning. So:

> 21 **It would have been better for them not to have known the way of righteousness**, than to **have known it** and then to turn their backs on the sacred command that was passed on to them.

Christians who have known the way of righteousness, but have turned their backs on God's sacred command would be better off not to have known Jesus at all. And next Peter gives a graphic picture of what they are like to God:

> 22 Of them the proverbs are true: **"A dog returns to its vomit,"** and, **"A sow that is washed goes back to her wallowing in the mud."**

These proverbs tell us that Christians who desert Jesus and return to a life of sin are just like dogs that return to eat the vomit they had just gotten rid of. Sickening? Yes! But that is what God thinks about those who deliberately return to their sin after being washed by the blood of Jesus.

They are also like "a sow that is washed and goes back to her wallowing in the mud." They once were cleansed and saved by the blood of Jesus, but now, like a pig that returns to wallow in the mud, they are as filthy with their sin as before they came to know Jesus. Only now they have the added sins of trampling the Son of God under foot and treating His blood as an unholy thing. How shameful, tragic and sad. They are indeed "worse off at the end than they were at the beginning."

Undeniable but Often Abused Passages

The sheer clarity of the above scriptures creates a puzzling question. What puzzles many who believe in Conditional Security is why so many otherwise solid Christians so tenaciously cling to a doctrine that the Scriptures so clearly contradict. However, those who believe once saved, always saved do have some very logical reasons for believing as they do, as we will see in chapter 14.

PART III

"ONCE SAVED, ALWAYS SAVED"

CHAPTER 14

Five Reasons They Believe What They Believe

Although I have never believed once saved, always saved, I have talked with many who do…or at least did. I also have read a lot of material written by those who accept this doctrine. So, please understand that my conclusions as expressed in this chapter are based solely on what I have learned from them.

As a result, I have found that most who adhere to this doctrine have very logical reasons for believing as they do. Here are five of the most obvious ones:

Reason #1: That's What They Have Always Believed

Many Christians believe once saved, always saved simply because that is what they have always believed. They came to the Lord through others who believed this way and they have gone to churches that teach this doctrine. As a result, it is difficult for them to accept anything that contradicts what they have always been taught.

This creates a problem. When they come to scriptures that contradict what they believe, they must conclude that such scriptures mean something other than what they clearly say, or they must write them off as too difficult to understand. The problem is then intensified by those who try to make such scriptures say something other than what they clearly mean.

Despite these tendencies, many who believe once saved, always saved are sincere Christians who truly love Jesus. It is most unfortunate that the once saved, always saved doctrine distorts their understanding of the many verses and passages that contradict this belief.

Reason #2: A Large Number of People Accept and Teach the Once Saved, Always Saved Doctrine

Some Christians are confident this teaching is correct because so many Christians accept and teach it. However, what the multitudes do or believe is never an indication that something is right.

In Numbers, chapters 13-14, Moses sent a leader from each of the 12 tribes of Israel to explore the land God was giving them. When the leaders came back, only two out of twelve gave a good report, citing God's will for them to go into the land. The rest discouraged the people from taking possession of the land, because of the difficulties that seemed to lie before them.

The majority of these leaders used human reasoning, which kept the people from doing God's will. As a result, the Israelites paid a heavy price for listening to the majority instead of what God was saying through His steadfast servants, Joshua and Caleb. Joshua and Caleb were fixed on what God said, but the majority were looking at circumstances. Going with God's Word, rather than the majority, is always the best way to go.

Five Reasons They Believe What They Believe

Reason #3: Fear for the Souls of Loved Ones

This is another powerful motivation to cling to the once saved, always saved doctrine. Many Christians have loved ones who once received Jesus, but have since turned from Him. It is very difficult for anyone to deal with the thought that their loved ones may end up in hell. Understandably, it is much more comforting to believe once saved, always saved, than to deal with the eternal loss of someone you love.

However, going with the desire to feel comfortable over what God's Word says is exactly what may cost a loved one their eternity with God. Believing something false prevents people from telling the truth to those who desperately need it. Isn't it better to warn those in a boat that is drifting towards a waterfall than to lead them to believe there is no waterfall to worry about? All that will do is cause them to feel comfortable and secure as they head for eternal disaster.

I would not want to be guilty of giving Christians who have chosen sin over Jesus false comfort while they are in danger of the fires of hell. I would much rather pray that God open their eyes to see their dangerous state and warn them before it is too late. I would rather snatch them from the boat of false security than allow them to go to their eternal destruction.

Reason #4: The Desire to Feel Secure

I do believe that God wants those who follow Jesus to feel secure in their salvation. But feeling secure while participating or living in sin is not what God intended. I have always believed that Christians who choose to desert Jesus are also choosing to forfeit their salvation; however, I have never felt insecure in my salvation. I know I am eternally secure as I remain in Jesus, who is my security and my salvation.

There are those who want to feel eternally secure while living in sin. However, how we want to feel should never

147

supersede what God's Word clearly says. Feelings can be misleading.

Paul wrote the following verse to the Philippian Christians:

> Phil. 2:12
> Therefore, my dear friends, as you have always obeyed —
> not only in my presence, but now much more in my
> absence — continue to **work out your salvation with fear
> and trembling...**

Although God's Word clearly commands us to work out our salvation with fear and trembling, many Christians have difficulty relating "work" to "salvation." Many also feel that once they are saved they have nothing to fear or tremble about, no matter how they live afterward.

As a result of the apparent conflict between what this verse says and what they believe, some say things such as, "In the Greek, this word 'fear' actually means reverence." I have heard this many times. However, it would make no sense for Paul to tell Christians to work out their salvation with reverence and trembling. How does reverence produce trembling? The word "reverence" simply means: "A feeling of profound respect" (WordWeb Dictionary).

In the Greek, the word "fear" in Philippians 2:12 actually means…"FEAR"! Here is the Strong's Concordance number and definition:

NT:5401 **phobos** (fob'-os); from a primary phebomai (to be put in fear); alarm or fright: *KJV* - be afraid, + exceedingly, fear, terror. [Phobos is where we get our word, "phobia."] (Strong's Greek/Hebrew)

Therefore, Phil. 2:12 makes it clear that what Christians do or don't do in this life can indeed affect their salvation. If it didn't, God's instruction to work out your salvation with fear and trembling would make no sense. God wants Christians to

Five Reasons They Believe What They Believe

know that they need to fear the consequences of indulging in willful sin. No one should feel eternally secure while living in a way that is offensive to God. And that's why Paul gave the Galatians this warning:

> Gal. 5:21
> **…I warn <u>you</u>, as I did before, that those who live like this** [in sin] **<u>will not inherit the kingdom of God</u>.**

Many who believe once saved, always saved do hate and seek to avoid sin, as they should. However, I have met more than a few Christians who, because they believe their salvation cannot be forfeited, sin freely with no fear of God at all.

It is tragic that there are so many teachers who have no qualms about telling those who are living in willful sin that they are still saved because of a past moment of faith. Instead, they should warn these careless Christians that, unless they repent, they are in danger of being cut off from Jesus, thrown into the fire and burned. We too should make every effort to deter such people from the disastrous direction they are headed.

Those who love Jesus are not perfect, but they do hate sin and seek to avoid it. Such Christians are eternally secure. They live in the peace, love and joy of the Lord and have no reason to fear for their salvation. However, those who live in willful sin and disobedience have plenty of reason to fear for their salvation (Rom. 2:8).

Now let's get to the last, but greatest, reason people believe any wrong doctrine:

Reason #5: Failing to Test All Things With All of God's Word

I have noticed that cashiers will occasionally hold certain bills up to the light to make sure they are legit. They know what a real bill is supposed to look like, which enables them to spot a phony when it shows up. This precaution prevents them from getting stuck with something counterfeit.

If only all Christians would do the same with the things of the Spirit. Christians failing to hold every teaching up to the light of God's Word as a whole is the reason for so much doctrinal error.

We must take an objective look at everything God's Word says about any doctrine that comes our way, no matter who is teaching it. And so, the question must be, "What does God's Word say, <u>in its entirety</u>, about the once saved, always saved doctrine?" And that is what this book is all about…comparing the once saved, always saved doctrine with God's Word. I have been comparing this doctrine with God's Word for many years and have found it to be long on man's "wisdom" and short on God's truth.

I have given you five reasons sincere Christians would believe the once saved, always saved doctrine. I am sure there are more, but these are the most notable ones to me. However, knowing why they believe as they do is not near as important as understanding what they believe and how these beliefs err in light of the Scriptures.

CHAPTER 15

"Once Saved, Always Saved" Beliefs and Teachings

While teaching in a foreign country, I was told not to order beef because you could never tell what you might be eating. The only way to be sure was to check out the kitchen to see if what was on the menu was actually in the kitchen. Those who didn't, like many Christians, would end up swallowing any strange thing put in front of them.

In Matthew 22:23-29, the Sadducees came to Jesus with a foolish question that was meant to trip Him up. After presenting their question, Jesus corrected these Sadducees by saying, "You are in error because you do not know the Scriptures or the power of God." Not only did Jesus nail their problem, but also the problem of all who embrace any wrong doctrine.

Naturally, not all who believe once saved, always saved believe exactly the same, for there are some variations in each person's belief system. Since there are so many variations, I will only address their three most common beliefs, along with a brief examination of each in the light of the Holy Scriptures.

Please understand that it is not my intention nor desire to demean those who believe once saved, always saved in any way. I am aware that many who believe this doctrine may be better Christians than I am in many ways. However, due to the harm any inaccurate doctrine can cause, it is my hope that God will use this book to bring the truth to light and to curb the acceptance of this doctrine. I have personally seen how harmful this teaching can be to weaker Christians who use this doctrine as a license to sin. Some who do this have given Jesus and His church a bad name among unbelievers. As a result, the hypocrisy these unbelievers see causes them to reject Jesus at their eternal expense.

Besides, this doctrine is not at all in sync with God's Word. Any part of any teaching that is out of sync with God's Word will eventually cause harm in some way.

Here is what I believe to be three of the once saved, always saved most basic beliefs, or teachings, along with my comments:

Teaching #1: Once a person has a moment of true faith in Jesus Christ, he will always remain saved and cannot again be lost. Such a person is "eternally secure."

Let's take a quick look at one of the passages used to support this doctrine:

> 1 John 5:11-13
> 11 And this is the testimony: **God has given us eternal life**, and **this life is in his Son**.
> 12 **He who has** [Greek: "is having"] **the Son has life**; he who does not have [Greek: "is not having"] the Son of God does not have life.
> 13 **I write these things to you who believe** [Greek: "are believing"] **in the name of the Son of God so that you may know that you have eternal life.**

Those who believe once saved, always saved refer to this, and other passages like it, to say that those who have received the Son are given eternal life. I absolutely agree. However, they go on to say something like, "Being that eternal life is forever, it cannot end. And if it cannot end, it makes sense that it cannot be forfeited or lost no matter how a person lives in the future." This conclusion is contrary to God's Word.

"Once Saved, Always Saved" Beliefs and Teachings

Notice the Greek tenses in the brackets included in the verses above. The original Greek uses what in English is called the "present continuous tense," which tells us that something is presently and continuously happening. And so, these verses actually tell us that it is those who are presently and continuously believing who can be sure they have eternal life, which is only found "in the Son." Jesus does not guarantee eternal life to those who once believed, but have since deserted Him.

That's why 1 John 5:13 does <u>not</u> say, "I write these things to you who once believed in the name of the Son of God, so you may know that you will have eternal life, no matter how you live in the future." You will not find such teaching anywhere in God's Word.

I know I have eternal life because I believe in and follow Jesus <u>now</u>. I am also keenly aware of how foolish it would be to abandon Jesus, for eternal security can only be found in Him.

I would also like to point out that the same John who tells us that eternal life is in the Son (1 John 5:11), also quotes Jesus telling us that those who do not "remain" in Him, will be "cut off, thrown into the fire and burned" (John 15:5-6). Therefore a Christian can forfeit his or her salvation by failing to remain in Jesus.

Teaching #2: If a professing Christian permanently turns away from Jesus, such a Christian was never really saved in the first place...no matter how strong his or her testimony for Jesus was before falling away.

It is easy to understand why this teaching would make sense to those who believe once saved, always saved...even though it cannot be found anywhere in the Bible. If they believe that it is impossible to completely fall away, what else can they say about those who do? They must conclude that Christians who fall away were never saved in the first place.

"Eternal Security" or "Eternal Insecurity?"

The idea that Christians who abandon Jesus were never saved in the first place seems to contradict the Doctrine of Eternal Security. It's more like the "Doctrine of Eternal Insecurity," and here's why. We must conclude from this teaching that a person can think he is a Christian on his way to heaven, but might not be. He can even live for a long period of time as a Christian, and then come to find out he was never really saved in the first place, since he turned from Jesus to a life of sin without repentance.

It is like being on the Jesus-ship to heaven with a friend. You invited your friend on this wonderful eternal cruise and introduced him to the Captain. He joyfully confessed the Captain as his Master and got on board. Your friend looked like he was on the ship, sat in the same seats you did, ate the same food, breathed the same air, and was as excited about the trip and its destination as you were. But, because he abandoned ship to jump back into the sea of sin, you are told that your friend was never on the ship in the first place. Rather confusing, isn't it?

If this could happen to someone else, how can you be sure it will not happen to you? If your friend was sure he was on the Jesus-ship to heaven, but later found out he never was, the same thing could happen to anyone who thinks he is saved. Not only does this make no sense, but it offers no real security at all… and, as I have already said, this teaching cannot be found anywhere in the Bible and, therefore, is unbiblical.

On the other hand, although I believe in Conditional Security, I know I am eternally secure as I "remain" in Jesus Christ, which will always result in bearing fruit for His glory (John 15:1-6). The condition to Conditional Security is simply that you remain in Jesus, the "True Vine," who will bring you from this world into eternity.

If I do fail and sin, I know God will forgive me as I confess and repent of my wrongdoing, but I never take sin lightly. I remain steadfastly on the Jesus-ship because I am aware of how dangerous it would be to jump ship for a life of sin. It is tragic that so many Christians jump overboard for a willful swim in the sea of sin, because they have been told they can't drown. It is a horrible thing to lead a person to believe it is impossible to drown, when it is very possible, and the once saved, always saved doctrine does just that.

An Even Greater Problem With This Teaching

Knowing that a Christian can fall away from Jesus and again be lost is a powerful motivator to avoid sin and pursue holiness as God commands (Heb. 12:14). But what is the motivator for weak Christians who believe their salvation is secured no matter how they live?

Many who believe once saved, always saved avoid sin simply because they love Jesus, which is the way it should be. However, there are also many less mature Christians who have a stronger pull towards this world than others. Knowing that the consequences of sin are much greater than just losing rewards or certain blessings may be just what they need to discourage them from taking sin lightly.

In view of what Jesus taught in John 15:5-6, I would not hesitate to tell Christians who have fallen away that they are in grave danger of being cut off from Jesus and will end up in hell unless they repent. Of course this should be done in love and out of a sincere concern for their eternity. I can also tell them that, because of their willful sin, they are trampling the Son of God under foot and treating the blood of Jesus as an unholy thing, which will result in a more severe punishment (Heb. 10:26-29). You will never hear this kind of powerful biblical prodding from someone who believes that a Christian cannot forfeit his or her salvation.

I was recently told of a distraught mother who shared a concern about her wayward son at a small-group gathering. Of course, the person who shared this gave no names, which was appropriate. This young man had once sincerely received Jesus, but has since turned his back on Him to live an immoral lifestyle. And, to make things worse, he had come to the point of even denying the existence of God.

In response to this mother's concern, a group leader told her, in so many words, "Don't worry about it…as long as he once received Jesus, he's still going to heaven…he can't lose his salvation."

How tragic! This young man was trampling the Son of God under foot and treating the blood of Jesus as an unholy thing (Heb. 10:26-29), yet his concerned mother was told that he was still going to heaven. What he really needed was prayer for repentance and a good, firm, loving warning from his mother, or from anyone else who was willing to tell him the truth. However, this leader softened the urgency of the matter by telling this mother that her son is still going to heaven.

Situations like this are not uncommon. Just this week I was talking to a Christian who once led a Bible study, but had not been attending church for quite some time. He was using some very foul language, but when salvation was brought up, he said with a big smile, "I can't lose my salvation…God has no stepchildren." This is something I have heard many times. He felt secure in His salvation, however, he showed no concern for his pathetic spiritual condition nor for the shame he was bringing to Jesus.

It is sad that many Christians who use this doctrine as a license to sin will be eternally lost, simply because they were made to feel secure in their sinful lifestyle. This could be avoided if they were taught what Jesus really said about turning from Him to a life of sin.

Teaching #3: The good or bad a Christian does cannot affect his salvation.

To many who believe once saved, always saved, obedience is a good work and lying, stealing and adultery are bad works.

Therefore, being that we are saved by grace, through faith, and not by works (Eph. 2:8-9), they believe that the good or bad we do cannot affect our salvation and eternity.

Let's see what the Bible says about this, while answering some important questions:

<u>Can a Christian Who Continues to Do Wrong End Up Being a Child of the Devil?</u>

What do the Scriptures say about those who willfully continue to do wrong?

> 1 John 3:10
> **This is how we know who the children of God are** and **who the children of the devil are: Anyone who does not do what is right [Greek: "is not doing right"] is not a child of God**; nor is anyone who does not love his brother.

According to Young's Literal Translation, "anyone who is not doing right," is more in sync with the Greek in this verse. This verse is not talking about those who at times stumble into sin, as we all do. It is talking about the person who willfully does wrong on a regular basis without remorse or repentance.

This verse also makes it clear that how I choose to live definitely defines me as "a child of God" or "a child of the devil." The Christian who chooses to live in sin cannot continue to be a child of God. Unless he repents, he will go from being a child of God to being a child of the devil.

Those who have once received Jesus, but then choose to live in sin are walking on dangerous ground and are headed for a possible change of spiritual fathers. This may be a hard thought for some to swallow, however, 1 John 3:10 is what God's Holy Word says.

The Gospel Truth

Is Jesus the Source of Eternal Salvation for Those Who Disobey Him?

The following passage is another portion of Scripture that is in conflict with the idea that how we live our lives after receiving Jesus has nothing to do with our salvation. Let's take a look at it and see what God says about obedience and salvation:

> Heb. 5:8-9
> 8 Although he was a son, he learned obedience from what he suffered
> 9 and, once made perfect, he became **the source of eternal salvation for all who obey him…**

Works cannot get us saved, but our obedience (or disobedience) has a lot to do with our salvation.

If Jesus is "the source of eternal salvation for all who obey Him," what of those who once received Him, joyfully believed for a while, but then turned to a life of disobedience (Luke 8:13)? The Bible never teaches that Jesus is the source of eternal salvation for Christians who willfully live in disobedience to Him.

Can a Christian Live by Faith and in Disobedience at the Same Time?

The Bible tells us, "The righteous will live by faith." That is the same as saying the righteous will live in obedience:

> Rom. 1:5
> Through him and for his name's sake, we received grace and apostleship to **call people** from among all the Gentiles **to the obedience that comes from faith.**

Notice that God's call on our life is "to the obedience that comes from faith." One of God's grand purposes of faith is to produce obedient followers. Those who once knew Jesus, yet have deserted Him for a life of willful disobedience no longer know (have a saving relationship with) Jesus. If they say they do, God says they are liars:

> 1 John 2:4
> **The man who says, "I know him," but does not do what he commands is a liar**, and the truth is not in him.

If faith is the tree, then obedience is the fruit—the fruit that God has desired since the Garden of Eden. God has made obedience possible by giving the Holy Spirit and a new nature to those who put their faith in Jesus as their Lord and Savior. Anyone who says they know Jesus, but does not produce this fruit may fool men, but they will never fool God.

Do Those Who Willfully Disobey Jesus Love Jesus?

> John 14:23-24
> 23 Jesus replied, "**If anyone loves me, he will obey my teaching**. My Father will love him, and we will come to him and make our home with him.
> 24 **He who does not love me will not obey my teaching**. These words you hear are not my own; they belong to the Father who sent me."

This verse should need no explanation. Jesus tells us that the person who is living in disobedience to God's Word simply does not love Him. This is the way Jesus looks at it, and we have no right to look at it differently. How can those who once received Jesus but now live in disobedience still be saved when, according to Jesus, they do not even love Him? Listen to what Paul said about those who do not love Jesus:

> 1 Cor. 16:22

If anyone does not love the Lord — a curse be on him. Come, O Lord!

There are many, many other verses that prove that our actions and choices can affect our salvation, but the above should suffice.

Although the once saved, always saved teachings we have covered in this chapter are not in sync with God's Word, there are still a good number of scriptures that those who teach this doctrine use to support what they believe. So the question is, "How can they have so many scriptures to support this doctrine if it is not biblical?" A close examination of these scriptures, in context, will answer this question.

CHAPTER 16

"Once Saved, Always Saved" Most Used Verses

Our society just doesn't want to live by the rules. If you don't believe me, just park by a stop sign anywhere in your city. If your city is anything like mine, you will see only two or so out of ten people come to a complete stop and, occasionally, some of them won't even slow down. And what about the cell phone law? Just yesterday, someone in church told me her elderly father was in the hospital with a broken neck because someone went through a stoplight while talking on her cell phone. Talking on the cell phone while driving has been against the law where I live for several years.

Rules are important for our own safety, and below are two that will protect any Christian from harmful misinterpretations of the Bible.

Two Important Rules for Proper Biblical Interpretation

I believe that if every Bible student would adhere to the following two simple rules, far fewer Christians would embrace erroneous doctrines.

Rule #1: **Never allow preconceived beliefs to determine the meaning of the text, but, rather, allow the text (in context) to change or determine your beliefs.**

Some Christians refuse to change their beliefs no matter what the Bible says. As a result they find themselves working hard to manipulate the clear meaning of the Scriptures to make them fit what they insist on believing.

Because the Pharisees did this, Jesus warned His disciples about their teaching (Matt. 16:12), which He likened to "yeast." In the same way that a little yeast will affect the whole batch of dough, a little wrong teaching can taint your understanding of God's Word as a whole.

So it is important that all Christians come to their doctrinal conclusions based on what God's Word says and not solely on what some denomination, teacher, or supposed biblical scholar says. The Scriptures should determine doctrine and not the other way around.

<u>Rule #2</u>: Remember that one verse, or portion of verses, in the New Testament does not cancel out another. Both must be embraced to arrive at a truly biblical conclusion.

If Johnny, who always tells the truth, said he saw a cat on the lawn, but later said he saw a dog on the lawn, that does not mean that a cat was not on the lawn. It simply means that both a cat and a dog were on the lawn.

However, coming to such simple conclusions about salvation can be difficult for some who embrace the once saved, always saved doctrine. I have noticed that when certain verses or passages clearly contradict verses that seem to support what they believe, they have difficulty accepting both at face value.

For instance, I have occasionally questioned acquaintances who believe once saved, always saved about John 15:1-6. Most simply refused to believe that Jesus was talking about Christians when He said that any branch <u>in Him</u> that does not bear fruit is in danger of being "cut off…thrown into the fire and burned" (verses one and six). They could not accept that these branches could be Christians although Jesus made it clear that these branches were <u>in Him</u>. Every Christian should know that only

Christians can be in Jesus, and nowhere in the Bible are non-Christians considered to be in Him. However, their existing belief makes it difficult for them to accept this important truth spoken by Jesus Himself.

When various texts seem to contradict each other, we must believe and teach them both…even if we do not yet understand how they work together. If you take this approach, the Holy Spirit will, in time, show you how beautifully such verses harmonize and compliment each other.

The fact that Jesus said His sheep shall never perish and that no one can snatch them from the Father's hand (John 10:28-29) does not cancel out or negate the fact that Jesus also said those who are in Him, but do not bear fruit, are in danger of being cut off, thrown into the fire and burned. Both statements are true, because Jesus taught both. (See chapters 5 and 6 for more in-depth teaching on how beautifully these verses fit together.)

Those who teach the once saved, always saved doctrine all use some of the same scriptures to support this belief. So let's apply the two rules for proper biblical interpretation (pages 161-162) as we examine the following scriptures.

"ONCE SAVED, ALWAYS SAVED" MOST USED VERSES

We are after God's truth. Therefore, as we examine the following passages, we will seek to answer these two questions: "Does the Word of God really say what the once saved, always saved doctrine says it does?" and "Is this doctrinal position really the result of God's truth or is it the result of human reasoning?"

Let's examine the following propositions to find out:

Jesus Will Never Drive Anyone Away

John 6:37

All that the Father gives me will come to me, and **whoever comes to me I will never [Greek: "absolutely not"] drive away**.

I have talked with many Christians who seem to interpret this verse as though Jesus said, "I will never drive away those who have known me, yet have abandoned me for a life of sin." Of course, Jesus didn't say that. Neither did He say that a person cannot walk away from Him of their own free will.

When a person comes to Jesus for new life and forgiveness, He <u>absolutely will not</u> drive that person away. It is important to see that the word "never" in this verse is a poor translation, for it focuses on the amount of time, while the Greek focuses on the strength of the promise...Jesus absolutely will not turn away anyone who comes to Him for life. He readily accepts all who come to and receive Him as their Lord and Savior.

For a more balanced biblical conclusion, let's not forget that Jesus also said He will "disown" (or deny) those who "disown" Him (Matt. 10:1-33). You cannot disown something that was not yours in the first place. Therefore, Jesus is talking about disowning those who once belonged to Him. Jesus will not drive away any who come to Him, yet He will disown those who belong to Him as a result of their first disowning Him.

<u>It is God's Will That Jesus Shall Lose None of All the Father Has Given Him</u>

Jesus said:

John 6:39
"And this is **the will of him who sent me**, that I shall **lose none** of all that he has given me, but raise them up at the last day."

This seems like a very convincing scripture for the once saved, always saved doctrine...that is if we take it out of context while ignoring the tenses. So let's consider this verse in context while inserting the Greek tenses used in the Young's Literal Translation for a more accurate understanding of what God is saying:

John 6:35-40
35 Then Jesus declared, **"I am the bread of life**. He who comes [Greek: 'is coming'] to me will never go hungry, and he who believes [Greek: 'is believing'] in me will never be thirsty.
36 But as I told you, you have seen me and still you do not believe.
37 All that the Father gives me will come to me, and whoever comes [Greek: 'is coming'] to me I will never drive away.
38 For I have come down from heaven not to do my will but to do the will of him who sent me.
39 **And this is the will of him who sent me, that I shall lose none of all that he has given me**, but raise them up at the last day.
40 **For my Father's will is that everyone who looks to [Greek: 'is beholding'] the Son and believes [Greek: 'is believing'] in him shall have eternal life, and I will raise him up at the last day."**

Jesus starts this passage off by declaring Himself to be the Bread of Life. It is interesting that He likens Himself to the manna from heaven that God gave the Israelites (Exodus Chapter 16). The Israelites had to continue to gather the manna each day to live, just as we must continue to believe in and follow Jesus to enjoy the life He gives.

In verse 35, notice that the Young's Literal Translation rightly uses the present continuous tense: "is coming to me" and "is believing in me." He also uses "is coming" in verse 37 while referring to those He will never drive away. And in verse 40, He makes it clear that it is he who "is beholding" and "is believing" that shall have eternal life and be raised up in the last day…not those who once came, once beheld, and once believed and then turned from the faith.

Remember that Jesus also said, "he who stands firm **to the end** will be saved" (Matt. 24:10-13) not "he who once believed will be saved no matter how he lives afterward." Jesus never attributes salvation to a one-time experience of true faith regardless of how a person lives afterward.

Of course, some will say, "What about verse 39 and 40 where Jesus said that it is the Father's will that He shall lose none that come to Him?" In response, I ask, "Does that mean God's will is always done?" For instance, the Bible tells us that God is not wanting anyone to perish, but everyone to come to repentance (2 Peter 3:9). Have all come to repentance? Are none going to perish?

Is it God's will that you sin? Of course not. Yet we all stumble in many ways (James 3:2), even though "His divine power has given us everything we need for life and godliness…" (2 Peter 1:3). The tempter is constantly tempting us, and sometimes we choose sin over God's will. At those times, it is our will over God's will. Thank God for His gracious forgiveness that is extended to those who confess (1John 1:9) and repent!

Although Jesus will never drive away any who are believing in and coming to Him, those who turn away from Him to live in sin without repentance will forfeit their salvation.

No One Can Be Snatched Out of Jesus' Hand

> John 10:27-29
> 27 **My sheep listen to my voice**; I know them, and **they follow me**.
> 28 **I give them eternal life**, and they shall never perish; **no one can snatch them out of my hand**.
> 29 My Father, who has given them to me, is greater than all; no one can snatch them out of my Father's hand.

I have already committed all of chapter six to this passage, so I will not say much about it here. But as a reminder, I will say that Jesus qualifies those who cannot be snatched out of His hand as being those who are listening to His voice and following Him…not those who are ignoring His voice and following after sin (verse 27).

No One Can Separate Us From the Love of Christ

Rom. 8:35-39
35 **Who shall separate us from the love of Christ?** Shall **trouble** or **hardship** or **persecution** or **famine** or **nakedness** or **danger** or **sword?**
36 As it is written: "For your sake we face death all day long; we are considered as sheep to be slaughtered."
37 No, in all these things **we are more than conquerors through him** who loved us.
38 **For I am convinced that neither death nor life, neither angels nor demons, neither the present nor the future, nor any powers,**
39 **neither height nor depth, nor anything else in all creation, will be able to separate us from** the love of God that is in Christ Jesus our Lord.

What a beautiful portion of Scripture! This passage tells us that nothing in all creation can separate us from the love of God "that is in Christ Jesus our Lord." However, it does not tell us that we cannot separate ourselves from Jesus, which is where God's love is found and experienced. We certainly can… although God would still love us if we did. While writing to the Roman Christians, Paul warned:

Rom. 8:13-14

13 **For if <u>you</u> live according to the sinful nature, you will die**; but if by the Spirit you put to death the misdeeds of the body, you will live,

14 because **those who are led by the Spirit of God are sons of God**.

The "you" Paul is writing to in these verses are Christians. And so Paul tells us that Christians can bring spiritual death (separation from God) upon themselves by living according to the sinful nature...

Paul also told these Galatian Christians:

Gal. 6:7-8

7 Do not be deceived: **God cannot be mocked. A man reaps what he sows.**

8 **The one who sows to please his sinful nature, from that nature will reap destruction**; the one who sows to please the Spirit, from the Spirit will reap eternal life.

Here Paul tells us that God cannot be mocked (treated with contempt). So Christians who "mock" God by living to please the sinful nature will "reap destruction" rather than experiencing the love of God.

Paul also tells these Galatian Christians that:

Gal. 5:19-21

19 **The acts of the sinful nature are obvious**: sexual immorality, impurity and debauchery;

20 idolatry and witchcraft; hatred, discord, jealousy, fits of rage, selfish ambition, dissensions, factions

21 and envy; drunkenness, orgies, and the like. **I warn <u>you</u>**, as I did before, **that those who live like this will not inherit the kingdom of God.**

Paul warns the Galatian Christians that if they choose to live in sin, they will not inherit the Kingdom of God. Not that God does not love Christians who have fallen away, but those who choose sin over Jesus will not be allowed into His kingdom, where the fullness of God's love is experienced.

You can be sure that the Holy Spirit will do everything He can to bring Christians who have deserted Jesus back to Him. But you can also be sure that God will never tolerate willful sin, nor will He interfere with the Christian's will. Each person must choose to love Jesus. Forced love is no love.

Being that God's wonderful love can only be found and experienced in Christ Jesus our Lord, we cannot expect to enjoy the refreshing love of God while living in sin outside of Him. Jesus is the only fountain of God's love. We cannot drink of His love while away from Him, slurping up the polluted waters of this world. This kind of living, if continued, will eventually lead to ultimate separation from God, which is eternal death.

God's Gifts and Call Are Irrevocable

Rom. 11:28-29
28 As far as the gospel is concerned, they are enemies on your account; but as far as election is concerned, **they** [the Israelites] **are loved on account of the patriarchs,**
29 **for God's gifts and his call are irrevocable**.

Although these verses are talking about God's call to Israel, many Bible students wrongly apply them to the Christian's salvation. Quoting only verse 29, they say, "See, once you are saved, your salvation is 'irrevocable.'" Not only is this verse taken out of context, but those who do so fail to consider what Paul said to these believers right before telling them that God's gifts and call to the Jews are irrevocable:

Rom. 11:21-22
21 For **if God did not spare the natural branches** [the Jews], **he will not spare you** [the Christians Paul was writing to] **either.**

22 Consider therefore the kindness and sternness of God: sternness to those who fell, but **kindness to you, provided that you continue in his kindness. Otherwise, you also will be cut off**.

Paul warned these believers not to let it go to their head that they were saved and Israel, in general, was not. He also made it clear in verse 22 that if these believers did not continue in God's kindness, they would be cut off just as the Jews were because of their unbelief and disobedience.

This portion of Romans perfectly parallels John 15:1-6, where Jesus told His disciples that unfruitful Christians who failed to remain in Him would be cut off, thrown into the fire and burned. Therefore, those who conclude that Romans 11:29 is saying that salvation cannot be forfeited by turning away from Jesus are completely out of sync with the immediate context and many other passages in the Bible.

As always, the truth can only be found by taking all scriptures in context and in the light of God's Word as a whole.

God Will Complete the Work He Started in You

Phil. 1:6
being confident of this, that he who began a good work in you will carry it on to completion until the day of Christ Jesus.

It's comforting to know that God is the Potter and I am His clay. When I came to the Lord I willingly placed myself on His Potter's wheel as I surrendered my life to Him. Actually, there is no other way to truly come to Jesus.

Once we put ourselves in Jesus' hands, God begins His good work in us, shaping and molding us to become more like Jesus each day. And God will continue this work until the day we are with the Lord…that is unless we choose to crawl off the

"Once Saved, Always Saved" Most Used Verses

Potter's wheel to do our own sinful thing. That is a very foolish thing to do, but there are Christians who do just that.

I know many Christians who love the Lord, and I am very confident they will continue in Jesus until the day they are with Him. However, my confidence in them is no guarantee that they will never fall away. Only God knows who will continue in Jesus and who will not. There are times I have been shocked to find that certain Christians, who were once totally committed to Jesus, had deserted Him to follow after sinful lusts and worldly desires.

Christians Are Shielded by God's Power

> 1 Peter 1:3-5
> 3 Praise be to the God and Father of our Lord Jesus Christ! In his great mercy **he has given us new birth into a living hope** through the resurrection of Jesus Christ from the dead,
> 4 and into **an inheritance that can never perish, spoil or fade — kept in heaven for you**,
> 5 who **through faith are shielded by God's power** until the coming of the salvation that is ready to be revealed in the last time.

Here is a glorious promise for those "who through faith are shielded by God's power." But what of those who have wandered from the faith? Are they shielded by God's power? Will they receive the imperishable inheritance God intends for those who follow Jesus?

We must remember that all we receive from God comes by faith. The righteous not only come to Jesus by faith, but they must continue in Him by faith:

> Col. 1:22-23

22 But now he has reconciled you by Christ's physical body through death to **present you holy in his sight, without blemish and free from accusation—**
23 **if you continue in your faith**, established and firm, not moved from the hope held out in the gospel. This is the gospel that you heard and that has been proclaimed to every creature under heaven, and of which I, Paul, have become a servant.

As I have pointed out before, the condition for being presented before God holy in His sight, without blemish and free from accusation is that "you continue in your faith…"

The Bible contains many verses that express the possibility of wandering from the faith. In Luke 8:13 we find that some will believe for a while and then fall away. God's Word also tells us that it is possible to abandon the faith and to fall from grace (1 Tim 4:1; Gal 5:4-7). Therefore, Jesus warns that many will turn from the faith and that only he who stands firm to the end will be saved (Matt. 24:10-13). Those who are foolish enough to abandon Jesus, also abandon all the good that is in Him…and, therefore, they can expect none of God's glorious eternal blessings.

I am eternally secure as I remain in Jesus. I have entered God's only place of security and, by the grace and power of God, I am staying there. Knowing that it is possible for me to forfeit my salvation by choosing sin and this world over Jesus just makes me hate sin and cling to Jesus all the more.

However, I have never feared for my salvation, not because I never sin, but because I am in Jesus, who is my salvation. And, as surely as God's Spirit lives in and empowers me, I have no intention to abandon Jesus for anything Satan and this world has to offer.

Life in Jesus has been good, rich, and joyful. Falling into some sort of sin is like falling in the mud. When I do, I am glad to get out as quickly as I can and to be washed by the blood of Jesus as I confess my sins with a repentant heart. And I am thankful for His immediate and gracious forgiveness (1 John 1:9). Wise Christians avoid spiritual mud puddles…and they certainly don't live in them!

The Holy Spirit is the Believer's Seal and Guarantee

Here is a passage I repeatedly hear when discussing the once saved, always saved doctrine. Let's take a good look at it:

> 2 Cor. 1:21-22
> 21 Now it is God who **makes both us and you stand firm in Christ**. He anointed us,
> 22 set his seal of ownership on us, and put his Spirit in our hearts as a deposit, guaranteeing what is to come.

The above is from the New International Version. However, the New King James version translates this passage this way:

> 2 Cor. 1:21-22
> 21 Now He who **establishes** us with you in Christ and has anointed us *is* God,
> 22 who also has sealed us and given us the Spirit in our hearts as a guarantee.

The translation, "He who establishes you," is closer to the original Greek than "God who makes both us and you stand firm in Christ," and it gives us a much clearer understanding of the text. The word "establish" means: *1. To set up or found. 2. Set up or lay the groundwork for.*

In other words, it is God who has set up, founded, or laid the groundwork for your life in Christ. To say that God <u>makes</u> a person stand firm in Christ would be like saying that God controls the person's will, eliminating the possibility of him falling. Of course this is contrary to what the Scriptures say.

We must also consider:

Eph. 1:13-14
13 And you also were included in Christ when you heard
the word of truth, the gospel of your salvation. Having
believed, you were **marked in him with a seal, the
promised Holy Spirit,**
14 who is **a deposit guaranteeing our inheritance** until
the redemption of **those who are God's possession** —
to the praise of his glory.

These verses may seem to support the once saved, always
saved doctrine to some Christians. However, let's take a careful
look at these verses and harmonize them with other verses that
will give us a more balanced understanding of what God is
saying. And, as we do this, let's keep in mind that the most basic
rule for solid biblical interpretation is:

**Passage "A" + Passage "B" = Truth (even if it does not
seem to make sense to you).**

NOT

**Passage "A" + My preconceived belief = Passage "B"
cannot mean what it clearly says.**

So, to arrive at a more biblical conclusion, we will apply the
rule for solid biblical interpretation to the above verses in the
following way:

BECAUSE THE VERSE SAYS:

2 Cor. 1:21
Now He who **establishes** us [sets us up] with you in Christ
and has anointed us *is* God, NKJV

"Once Saved, Always Saved" Most Used Verses

Most who believe "once saved, always saved" conclude that if God establishes us in Christ, then nothing in this world can cause us to fall or forfeit our salvation and be cut off from Jesus.

But we must also consider these scriptures:

> John 15:5-6
> 5 **I am the vine; you are the branches.** If a man remains in me and I in him, he will bear much fruit; apart from me you can do nothing.
> 6 **If anyone does not remain in me, he is like a branch that is thrown away and withers; such branches are picked up, thrown into the fire and burned.**

Also see:
Matt. 7:24-27; 24:10-13; Luke 8:13; 1 Cor. 10:12; Gal. 5:4, 19-21; Heb. 4:11; 6:4-8; 2 Peter 1:10; 2:20-22; 3:17.

Therefore, the biblical conclusion must be that God does indeed establish us (set us up) in Christ (2 Cor. 1:21). However, that does not mean that God forces us to remain in and serve Christ. A Christian can turn away from the faith any time he or she is foolish enough to choose to. Those who do not remain in Jesus are in danger of being "cut off" from Jesus, "thrown into the fire and burned."

Christians who maintain a close, trusting and obedient relationship with Jesus have nothing to fear. They are eternally secure as they remain in Jesus. It is a foolish thing to abandon Jesus and all His wonderful blessings to live in sin.

BECAUSE THE VERSES SAY:

2 Cor. 1:22

[He/God] **set his seal of ownership on us**, and **put his Spirit in our hearts…**

Eph. 1:13-14
13 …you were **marked in him with a seal, the promised Holy Spirit,**
14 who is a deposit **guaranteeing our inheritance** until the redemption of **those who are God's possession** — to the praise of his glory.

Most who believe "once saved, always saved" conclude that if God has placed his seal of ownership upon us (the Holy Spirit), we belong to Him and cannot fall away at the expense of our salvation. We are His and nothing can change that. Because we are His, we are guaranteed a future inheritance and redemption.

But we must also consider these scriptures:

Rom. 11:21-22
21 For if God did not spare the natural branches, he will not spare you either.
22 **Consider** therefore **the kindness and sternness of God**: sternness to those who fell, but **kindness to you, provided that you continue in his kindness. Otherwise, you also will be cut off**.

Col. 1:22-23
22 But now he **has reconciled you** by Christ's physical body through death **to present you holy in his sight, without blemish and free from accusation—**
23 **if you continue in your faith**, established and firm, not moved from the hope held out in the gospel. **This is the gospel that you heard** and that has been proclaimed to every creature under heaven, and **of which I, Paul, have become a servant.**

"Once Saved, Always Saved" Most Used Verses

1 Tim 4:1
The Spirit clearly says that in later times **some will abandon the faith** and follow deceiving spirits and things taught by demons.

Also see:
Matt. 7:24-27; 24:10-13; Luke 8:13; John 15:1-5; 1 Cor. 10:12; Gal. 5:4,19-21; Heb. 4:11; 6:4-8; 2 Peter 1:10, 2:20-22; 3:17.

Therefore, the biblical conclusion must be that God has given us the Holy Spirit as His seal of ownership. We belong to Jesus, but not all who belong to Him will continue in Him, for some will abandon the faith to follow deceiving spirits. They will fail to continue in their faith and will grieve the Holy Spirit by their sinful life.

Having been sealed with God's Spirit does not mean that God has taken control of our will. We must continually choose to follow Jesus over the sinful nature. Those who do not continue in God's "kindness" are warned that they can be "cut off" from God's source of salvation.

Those who once bore the seal of the Holy Spirit, but have since turned to a life of sin "will not inherit the kingdom of God" (Gal. 5:19-21).

And so we see that the truth is found only when we take all verses together and harmonize them, without changing the clear meaning of any.

To take 2 Corinthians 1:21-22 and Ephesians 1:13-14 as saying, "Once you are in Jesus, you cannot be cut off from Him," would be saying that the Bible contradicts itself and that what Jesus said about fruitless Christians is not true.

Christians Who Fall Away Were Never Saved in the First Place

Although I have heard this said many times, I have never been given any scriptures that support this belief. That is because there are none. The reason this doctrine has become popular among those who believe once saved, always saved is that they do not know what else to conclude about those who have received Jesus as their Lord and Savior, but then deserted Him, even dying in a state of apostasy. If they admit that such people were once saved, they would also be acknowledging that it is possible for Christians to fall away at the expense of their salvation.

Actually, it was not until recently that I came across a website where someone used 1 John 2:19 to say that Christians who desert the Lord were never really saved in the first place. I have included verse 18 below so that you can see verse 19 in context.

1 John 2:18-19
18 Dear children, this is the last hour; and as you have heard that the antichrist is coming, **even now many antichrists have come**. This is how we know it is the last hour.
19 **They went out from us, but they did not really belong to us. For if they had belonged to us, they would have remained with us; but their going showed that none of them belonged to us.**

There are several things you should immediately notice about these verses:

1. These verses say nothing about falling from the faith.
2. These verses say nothing about salvation.
3. These verses say nothing about coming to or abandoning Jesus.

As a matter of fact, these verses have nothing at all to do with Christians or salvation. In verse 18, John makes it clear that verse 19 is talking about "antichrists" who had slipped in among them, but then left them, showing that they were really not a part of them in the first place. Antichrists are not Christians nor are they saved. Therefore, 1 John 2:19 is being used totally out of context to say that those who have fallen from the faith were never really saved in the first place. Of course the web site that used this verse did not include verse 18, which would have made it clear that John was talking about antichrists and not Christians.

Being that there are absolutely no verses or passages that support the teaching that if someone falls away from the Lord he or she was never really saved in the first place, we must conclude that this teaching is unbiblical. And, therefore, this teaching should not be taught by any conscientious Bible teacher, nor should it be accepted and passed on by believers.

CHAPTER 17

What Will Become of Sincere Christians Who Preach an Inaccurate Gospel?

I know and love many sincere Christians who have embraced the once saved, always saved doctrine. However, I have noticed that, as a result of this belief, they inadvertently misinterpret certain passages that contradict what they believe.

This is a serious problem. Inaccurately teaching God's Word for any reason can have serious consequences for those who teach and for the hearer. So the big question is: "What will become of sincere Christians who teach an inaccurate gospel?"

The answer to this question is found in 1 Corinthians 3:9-15. We will take one verse at a time to gain the most accurate understanding of God's intention for this passage:

1 Cor. 3:9-15
9 For **we are God's fellow workers; you are God's field, God's building**.

Having been a general contractor before becoming a pastor, I can relate to the importance of how a builder builds and the quality of the material he uses. How one builds and the quality of materials has a huge effect on the strength of the building. If a builder does shabby work with inferior material, that which he builds will not last as it should.

And so, in the above verse, Paul starts this passage off by pointing out that those who teach God's Word are God's fellow workers who are called to build up "God's building," which consists of the body of Christ. Therefore, the Apostle says:

10 By **the grace God has given** me, **I laid a foundation as an expert builder**, and **someone else is building on it. But each one should be careful how he builds.**
11 For **no one can lay any foundation other than the one already laid, which is Jesus Christ**.

Paul says that, by the grace of God, he laid the foundation as an expert builder. In other words, he taught those who had come to Jesus as carefully as an expert builder would build a house. And Paul was careful to lay the solid foundation of Jesus Christ, pointing to Him as the only source of salvation and life. All they would learn and do from this point would come with a continual focus on Jesus as their Master and Savior.

However, Paul knew that after he had established this Divine Foundation, others would have to continue the building process, and it was important that they built with good, solid, non-compromising teaching. This would enable these believers to stand strong through the trials and temptations of life…trials and temptations that are sure to come against all who are "God's building."

So, concerning this foundation, Paul said, "someone else is building on it, but each one should be careful how he builds." Paul's concern was not that these Christians would not be taught…his concern was how accurately other Christian workers would teach them. And so Paul says:

12 **If any man builds** on this foundation **using gold, silver, costly stones, wood, hay or straw**,

Notice that Paul lists different materials, starting with the best and working down to the worst and weakest. In other words, those who teach Christians must be careful to teach precisely what God's Word says. Pure and accurate teaching would be "gold, silver or costly stones" while inaccurate teaching would be "wood, hay or straw." The quality of each person's teaching is of eternal importance because:

> 13 **his work will be shown for what it is,** because the Day will bring it to light. It will be revealed with fire, and **the fire will test the quality of each man's work**.

The "day" will come when the quality of each person's teaching ("his work") will be shown for what it is. It will be shown by whether it gave spiritual strength or weakness to those being taught.

It is important to know that the word "Day" in the above verse, although capitalized, is not referring to the "Day of Judgment." Paul cannot be referring to the Day of Judgment here, because the Day of Judgment will result in the eternal fire of punishment. However, the day spoken of above is a day that "fire will test the quality of each man's work."

A day of testing is a lot different than a day of judgment. It is more like the day of evil spoken of in Ephesians 6:13, which is a time that will test the strength of Christians as they do spiritual battle. Well-taught, faithful Christians will be able to stand in the face of such trails and temptations. Once a person is out of this body, the times of testing are over and all that is left is eternal life or eternal death.

Every Christian we teach will face trials and temptations, and the material we build with will determine how well they will stand up against life's storms and Satan's deceptions and temptations. Teachers who build with gold, silver and costly-stone teachings are working with God to develop strong Christians who will stand firm when trials and temptations come. But teachers who build with wood, hay or straw will be the cause of many Christians falling in times of testing. So Paul tells us:

14 If what he has built survives, he will receive his reward.

When those who have been taught with the pure, unadulterated Word of God survive the fiery trials of life, those who taught them will receive their reward.

But what of those who teach with wood, hay and straw? What of those sincere teachers who taught the once saved, always saved doctrine to believers who took it as a license to sin and ended up falling away in times of testing?

15 If it is burned up, he will suffer loss; **he himself will be saved, but only as one escaping through the flames.**

Now that's a sobering thought. Paul says that inaccurate teaching can actually cause what Christian workers have built to be burned up. Now, remember that the builders (teachers) are called to build Christians (verse 9-12).

Many who have embraced the once saved, always saved doctrine will not do well when faced with fiery trials and temptations. Instead of repenting in the fear of the Lord, some will use this doctrine to comfort themselves in their sin. Believing they cannot forfeit or lose their salvation, they live in a false sense of security.

Those who use the once saved, always saved doctrine in this way are headed for a tragic eternity. The Bible warns that they are crucifying the Son of God all over again (Heb. 6:4-8). Jesus also warned that those who fail to bear good fruit will be cut off from Him, thrown into the fire and burned. This is a terrible loss that can often be avoided by teaching the truth.

In the light of the Scriptures, I must consider the once saved, always saved doctrine as "wood, hay or straw" teaching. Of course, there are many Christians who have embraced this doctrine who will fall when tested, but get up again and continue in the Lord. But then there are those who, because of this doctrine, will continue in their fallen state and will be "burned up" and lost forever.

How will that affect those sincere Christians who taught them this "straw" doctrine? Can you imagine the feelings of the sincere pastor, teacher, or Christian worker who had been teaching the once saved, always saved doctrine when he finds out that souls were lost for eternity because of what he taught or failed to teach? Yes, "he himself will be saved," but, indeed, it will be "as one escaping through the flames" (verses 14-15).

James tells us, "Not many of you should presume to be teachers, my brothers, because you know that we who teach will be judged more strictly" (James 3:1). How careful those who teach should be to share only the pure, unadulterated Word of God with God's people.

What every Christian does with God's truth can make the difference between eternal life and eternal death, which brings us to a most important question…"What would God have us do with what we have learned from His Word concerning the security of the believer?"

CHAPTER 18

Contending for the Faith

We live at a time when it is unpopular to confront others for immoral or improper actions and words. The popular belief of today is that everyone should be able to do their own thing, and others have no right to "judge" or correct them. What a mess this idea has created in our society and in our churches.

Sadly, many Christians have embraced this complacent attitude toward correcting others, and, as a result, sin and false doctrine in the church are seldom confronted and curbed.

However, the Bible tells us that:

2 Tim. 3:16-17
16 **All Scripture is** God-breathed and is **useful for** teaching, **rebuking, correcting** and training in righteousness,
17 so that the man of God may be thoroughly equipped for every good work.

2 Tim. 4:1-2
1 In the presence of God and of Christ Jesus, who will judge the living and the dead, and in view of his appearing and his kingdom, **I give you this charge:**
2 Preach the Word; be prepared in season and out of season; **correct, rebuke and encourage — with great patience and careful instruction**.

God tells us that His Word is not only to be used to teach and encourage, but also to "correct" and "rebuke." And in 2 Timothy 4: 3, He tells us why we must be faithful to use His Word to correct others who are in the wrong:

> 2 Tim. 4:3
> For the time will come when men will not put up with sound doctrine. Instead, to suit their own desires, they will gather around them a great number of teachers to say what their itching ears want to hear.

This prophetic writing began its fulfillment shortly after it was penned and has escalated to what is happening in churches today. There are presently a great number of teachers willing to say what itching ears want to hear, instead of telling the truth as revealed in God's Word.

This does not mean that, in the case of the once saved, always saved doctrine, everyone who teaches it does so for unethical reasons. On the contrary, most who teach this doctrine do so because they sincerely believe it.

However, many who embrace this doctrine inevitably end up altering the clear meaning of passages that contradict what they believe. And as a result, they pass their tainted understanding of the Scriptures on to those they share with. Sadly, this in turn distorts other people's knowledge of the Lord Jesus Christ and His Word. This is very serious. That is why God urges us to contend for the faith:

> Phil. 1:27
> Whatever happens, **conduct yourselves in a manner worthy of the gospel** of Christ. Then, whether I come and see you or only hear about you in my absence, I will know that you stand firm in one spirit, **contending as one man for the faith of the gospel...**

Contending for the Faith

Jude 3
Dear friends, although I was very eager to write to you about the salvation we share, I felt I had to write and **urge you to contend for the faith that was once for all entrusted to the saints.**

God has once for all entrusted the pure, unadulterated gospel to the saints. In case you don't already know it, the word "saint" in God's Word does not refer to some special person who has been designated a saint by the hierarchy of a church. In the New Testament, the word "saint" refers to anyone who believes in and follows Jesus Christ. This means you and me.

Therefore, God has given us the personal responsibility to "contend for the faith that was once for all entrusted" to us. That means we must contend for the same gospel Paul and the Apostles proclaimed. This is the gospel of redemption, forgiveness and reconciliation for those who were once alienated from God. This is the gospel that was initiated at the cross through Christ's physical body so that we can be presented "holy in His sight, without blemish and free from accusation." This also is the gospel with an "if" in it:

Col. 1:21-23
21 Once you were alienated from God and were enemies in your minds because of your evil behavior.
22 But now he has reconciled you by Christ's physical body through death to present you holy in his sight, without blemish and free from accusation—
23 **if you continue in your faith**, established and firm, not moved from the hope held out in the gospel. This is the gospel that you heard and that has been proclaimed to every creature under heaven, and of which I, Paul, have become a servant.

The gospel that has been entrusted to us includes the condition that all who have come to Jesus by faith must

189

"continue" in their faith to be presented to God without blemish and free from accusation. The good news is that Jesus has made salvation available to all who come to Him by faith… a faith that produces an obedient life:

> Rom. 1:5
> Through him and for his name's sake, we received grace and apostleship **to call people from among all the Gentiles to the obedience that comes from faith**.

The good news (gospel) is that we are totally and eternally secure in Jesus Christ, who is our only source of life, peace and hope. Those who abide in and follow Jesus can enjoy the most wonderful, joy-filled and glorious life imaginable. However, this same gospel also tells us that those who fail to remain in Jesus and return to a fruitless life of sin, are in danger of being cut off from Him, thrown into the fire and burned (John 15:1-6).

The good news of salvation and forgiveness was never intended to be a ticket to heaven for those who had once received Jesus, but have since discontinued their trusting and obedient relationship with Him. Those who have abandoned Jesus have also abandoned their salvation. This is a very dangerous situation to be in, and those who find themselves in it must never be allowed to think they are secure in Jesus while living in sin.

I am aware that the destiny of loved ones who have passed away while appearing to be in a fallen state is a serious concern. However, we must keep in mind that they are in God's hands… and He is gracious and ready to forgive and embrace those who sincerely repent, even at the last breath. Only God knows the eternal destiny of each person, but how foolish to wait in hopes of grasping for eternal life at the last breath.

The purpose of this book is to contend for the true gospel of Jesus Christ and to equip others to do the same. I pray you see the seriousness of this call, and I encourage you to read and understand this book in its entirety. I also encourage you to share this book with others, including those who believe once saved, always saved...they need to hear the truth. And whatever you share, be sure to share it in the love of Jesus.

May God bless you, fill you, and empower you with the Holy Spirit as you serve His Majesty, King Jesus!

SPECIAL REQUEST

Has this book helped you? Please leave an honest review on Amazon.com and help get the word out. It will only take a few moments.

God bless you richly in the wonderful name of Jesus!
Claude A. Short

Quick References:

1. It is our responsibility to "contend for the faith" (Jude 3).

2. It is dangerous to preach a gospel other than the one the Apostles preached (See Gal. 1:6-9).

3. The once saved, always saved doctrine teaches that once you have received Jesus there is no "if" (condition) to salvation. However, the Apostles proclaimed a gospel with an "if" in it. "If" is a conditional word that means: "On the condition that." The condition that must be met for final salvation is that "you continue in your faith" and "remain in Jesus." This admonition would be senseless if it were not possible to discontinue in the faith by abandoning Jesus. (Col. 1:21-23; John 15:1-6)

4. Therefore, Christian "brothers" are saved "if" they "hold firmly" to God's Word. Those who do not have "believed in vain." (1 Cor. 15:1-2)

5. This concept is much easier to accept and understand once we see that there are three stages to the Christian life:

Stage One - Coming to and receiving Jesus (John 1:12)

Stage Two - The Christian Journey of Life (1 Peter 2:11; 5:8-9; Rom. 8:13-14; 1 Tim. 6:12; Rom. 13:11-12)

Stage Three - Everlasting Life in Heaven (Mark 10:29-30; Jude 21)

6. Christians are not saved by works, but they are saved by grace to do good works (Eph. 2:8-10).

7. Therefore Paul tells us that it is Christians who persist "in doing good" as a result of their faith that will receive eternal life from God (Rom. 2:7-8).

8. Jesus tells us that it is those who stand firm to the end who will be saved (Matt. 24:12-13).

9. It is through Jesus, by faith that we have gained access into this grace in which we now stand (Rom. 5:1-2).

10. If we go to the original Greek, we can see more clearly that whoever presently "is believing" in Jesus is saved, not those who once believed and have since fallen away:

Young's Literal Translation:

John 3:16
for God did so love the world, that His Son — the only begotten — He gave, that every one who **is believing** in him may not perish, but may have life age-during. YLT

Quick References

John 3:18
he who is believing in him **is not judged**, but he **who is not believing hath been judged** already, because he hath not believed in the name of the only begotten Son of God. YLT

John 3:36
he who **is believing** in the Son, **hath life age-during**; and **he who is not believing** the Son, **shall not see life**, but the wrath of God doth remain upon him. YLT

John 6:40
and this is the will of Him who sent me, that every one who **is beholding the Son**, and **is believing** in him, **may have life age-during**, and I will raise him up in the last day. YLT

Acts 10:43
to this one do all the prophets testify, that through his name every one that **is believing** in him **doth receive remission of sins.** YLT

Rom. 1:16
for I am not ashamed of the good news of the Christ, for it is the power of God to **salvation to every one who is believing**, both to Jew first, and to Greek. YLT

1 John 5:11-13
11 and this is the testimony, that life age-during did God give to us, and this — the life — is in His Son;
12 **he who is having the Son, hath the life; he who is not having the Son of God — the life he hath not.**
13 These things I did write to you who are believing in the name of the Son of God, that ye may know that life ye have age-during, and that ye may believe in the name of the Son of God. YLT

11. Jesus tells us that eternal life is not just a matter of existing forever, but of having a personal relationship with Him (John 17:3). Living forever is the result of this relationship.

12. Therefore, we must know Jesus to have eternal life. The Bible tells us that those who say they know Him yet disobey Him are liars (1 John 2:3-4).

13. Thus, Christians who turn from Jesus to a life of sin "will not inherit the kingdom of God" (Gal. 5:19-21).

14. Many Christians believe we have to sin because we are still in the flesh. However, God's Word tells us that Christians "are no longer slaves to sin" (Rom. 6:9) and that we are to pursue holiness (Heb. 12:14) for Jesus. This does not mean we never sin, but that we are free from the power of sin. And the result is eternal life (Rom. 6:22).

15. Christians should never feel comfortable or secure while living in sin, but should "work out their salvation with fear and trembling" (Phil. 2:12). If Christians cannot forfeit their salvation, what is there to fear and tremble about? However, I have met many Christians who, because they believe once saved, always saved, sin freely with no fear of God.

16. The original Greek makes it clear that we can know we have eternal life only if we presently "are believing" (present continuous tense), not because we once believed (1 John 5:11-13; John 6:47).

17. It is clear that only those who "continue" in their faith will be presented to God, holy in His sight, without blemish and free from accusation (Col. 1:22-23).

Quick References

18. Also, it is possible for people who have believed for a while to abandon the faith and, thus, to fall from grace and be lost. It is also clear that only those who stand firm to the end will be saved. (1 Tim. 6:20-21; Luke 8:13; 1 Tim. 4:1; Gal. 5:4; Matt. 24:10-13)

19. The Christian who turns to a life of sin will go from being a child of God to being a child of the devil (1 John 3:10).

20. It is important to remember that Jesus is the "source of eternal salvation" for those who obey Him, not for those who once received Him but now live in disobedience (Heb. 5:8-9).

21. People can say they love Jesus all they want, but Jesus tells us that those who obey Him are the ones who love Him and that those who disobey Him do not love Him (John 14:21-24).

22. Those who do not love and obey Jesus are accursed (1 Cor. 16:22).

23. And those who do not live in obedience to Jesus do not live in Him who is the eternal life (1 John 3:24).

24. It is impossible for those who are presently born again to willfully live in sin without remorse and repentance. Those who were once saved, but feel no remorse for their sin should question their present state of salvation (1 John 3:9).

25. Our loving and caring God is also a just God. He will give to each person according to how they have chosen to live (Rom. 2:6-8; 1 Cor. 6:8-9; Gal. 5:21).

26. It is Important to see that no one can snatch the person who listens to Jesus' voice and follows Him out of His hand (John 10:27-29). However, those who once did, but no longer listen to and follow Jesus have walked out of His hand.

27. Christians who turn from Jesus to live according to the sinful nature "will not inherit the kingdom of God" (Rom. 8:13-14; Gal. 5:19-21; 6:7-8).

28. Although God's gifts and call to Israel are irrevocable, the Jews have, for the most part, been temporarily cut off from God's salvation because of their unbelief (Rom. 11:28-29).

29. God warns Christians that if they do not "continue in His kindness," they will be "cut off" from His source of salvation, just as the Jews were (Rom. 11:21-22).

30. Jesus warns us that "many will turn away from the faith" and that we must "stand firm to the end to be saved." Those who receive Jesus, but fall away without repenting, will not be saved (Matt. 24:10-13).

31. We must be careful to maintain a trusting and obedient relationship with Jesus so that we will not fall (1 Cor. 10:11-12).

32. Although we are marked "in Him" with the seal of the Holy Spirit, we must remain in Him to avoid being "cut off, thrown into the fire and burned" (Eph. 1:13-14, John 15:1-2, 5-6).

33. We must remember that eternal life can only be found in Jesus (1 John 5:11-12; Rom. 6:23).

34. Therefore, only those who remain in Jesus have eternal life, and not those who abandon Him for a life of sin (John 1:5-6; 1 John 5:12).

35. And so the gift of eternal life is not for those who receive and then abandon Him, but only for those who receive and "continue in Him" (1 John 2:28; Col. 2:6).

36. Jesus tells us that the Father will cut off every branch in Him (every Christian) that fails to bear fruit for His glory. They will then be "thrown into the fire and burned"…that is unless they repent and return to Jesus (John 15:1-2, 6).

37. Those who continue to live in sin without repentance are promised wrath and anger (Rom. 2:7-8).

38. Those who have escaped the corruption of the world by knowing Jesus, and then go back to it, are worse off than they were at the beginning. It would have been better for them not to have known Jesus, who is the way of righteousness, in the first place (2 Peter 2:20-22).

39. God calls and equips us for holiness, not for sinfulness (1 Peter 1:15-17).

40. Christians who are living in sin have good reason to fear the Lord (Heb. 10:26-31). Note that this warning is to those who have been sanctified by the blood of Jesus (verse 29) and, therefore, they must be born-again Christians.

41. The Galatian Christians were warned that living in sin would disqualify them for "the kingdom of God" (Gal. 5:19-21).

42. Christians who live for self and sin are likened to salt that loses its saltiness. The only way salt can lose its saltiness is by being chemically changed into something other than what it once was. Christians who become apostate are no longer what they once were… they have become ex-Christians who are no longer good for anything but to be trampled under foot by man (Matt. 5:13).

43. Christians who are not spiritually ready for Jesus' return will be locked out from His presence when He returns (Matt. 25:1-13).

44. Christians who do not use what God has given them for His glory will suffer eternal loss (Matt. 25:14-21).

45. God expects those who belong to Jesus to live for Him (1 Cor. 6:19-20).

46. Christians are instructed by God to do certain things that will make their calling and election sure (2 Peter 1:10-11).

47. There are those who will receive the gospel, "believe for a while," and then "fall away in the time of testing" (Luke 8:13).

48. Therefore, we are encouraged to "fight the good fight" while "holding on to the faith" in order to avoid shipwrecking our faith (1 Tim. 1:18-19).

49. Those who "abandon" the faith end up following "deceiving spirits and things taught by demons" (1 Tim. 4:1).

50. An eagerness for money can cause Christians to wander from the faith (1 Tim. 6:8-10).

51. Because of the possibility of forfeiting eternal life, Paul told Timothy: "Take hold of the eternal life to which you were called......" (1 Tim. 6:12).

52. For we share in Christ only if we hold firmly till the end the confidence we had at first (Heb. 3:14).

53. If God's word remains (stays) in us, we will remain (stay) in Jesus and receive His promise of eternal life (1 John 2:24-25).

54. John would not tell us to "continue in" Jesus if it were not possible to discontinue in Him (1 John 2:28).

Quick References

55. Jesus never would have told us that those who overcome will never have their names blotted out of the book of life, if it were not possible for our names to be blotted out of the book of life (Rev. 3:5). In the Old Testament we find that a person's name can definitely be blotted out of the book of life (Ex. 32:32-33).

56. Those who alter God's word are in grave danger of having their "share in the tree of life and the holy city" taken away, which means there will be no eternal life for them (Rev. 22:19).

57. A careful comparison between Paul's "wretched man" in Romans chapter 7 and the characteristics of the true Christian (Rom. 6 and 8) confirms that Paul's "wretched man" is a picture of one who is trying to live under the law or is living according to the sinful nature. Paul's "wretched man" is not a portrait of the normal Christian life, for this "wretched man" is still a slave to sin. It is those who are led by the Spirit, and not by the sinful nature who are the children of God (Rom. 8:13-14).

58. God sent Jesus to die for our sins and to free us from the power of the sinful nature (Rom. 8:3-4).

59. We all sin, but those who live by faith and by the indwelling power of the Holy Spirit will overcome their sin. God is able to do what we cannot do in ourselves (Eph 3:19-21).

60. Satan may get the best of us at times, but the normal Christian life is one of victory in Jesus by the power of His Spirit who gives "us everything we need for life and godliness" (2 Peter 1:3).

61. Those who have tasted [Greek: experienced] the heavenly gift of eternal life and have shared in the Holy Spirit must be, or have been, saved Christians. The Bible tells us that if they fall away, they are crucifying the Son of God all over again and

subjecting Him to public disgrace. As a result they are like "land that drinks in the rain" and then "produces thorns and thistles." In the end such land (fallen Christians) will be burned (Hebrews 6:4-8).

62. Predestination is based on God's foreknowledge. God simply chooses and predestines to eternal life those He foreknew would receive and follow Jesus to the very end. He also predestines to eternal damnation those He foreknew would abandon Jesus to live in sin (Rom. 8:29-30; 1 Peter 1:1-2).

63. Calvinism, and the idea that God would actually create certain people just to send them to hell without giving them a choice in the matter, should be totally rejected. The Bible tells us that God is "not wanting any to perish" and that He "wants all men to be saved and to come to a knowledge of the truth" (2 Peter 3:9; 1 Tim. 2:3-4).

64. Many sincere Christian workers who teach the "wood, hay or straw" doctrine of once saved, always saved inadvertently cause Christians who are living in sin to have a false sense of security in their salvation. As a result, many of these Christians will not repent and will end up being lost forever. Those sincere Christians who taught this doctrine will be saved, but "only as one escaping through flames" as they discover the destruction they have caused by their unsound doctrine (1 Cor. 3:9-15).

65. Therefore it is important that we cast out all preconceived beliefs that contradict God's Holy Word. Instead of trying to make God's Word fit our preconceived beliefs, we must study God's Word objectively. As we do, the Holy Spirit will faithfully reveal God's truth to us (2 Tim. 2:15, 4:20).

Made in the USA
San Bernardino, CA
30 August 2014